EDUCATOR'S GUIDE TO
Catholic Identity

Paul Sharkey

VAUGHAN PUBLISHING

Published in Australia by
Vaughan Publishing
32 Glenvale Crescent
Mulgrave VIC 3170
A joint imprint of The Broken Bay Institute and Garratt Publishing

Copyright © 2015 Paul Sharkey
All rights reserved. Except as provided by Australian copyright law,
no part of this publication may be reproduced in any manner
without prior permission in writing from the publisher.

Cover design by Canary Graphics

The author and publisher gratefully acknowledge the permission granted to reproduce
the copyright material in this book. Every effort has been made to trace copyright holders
and to obtain their permission for the use of copyright material.

The publisher apologises for any errors or omissions in the above list and would be grateful
if notified of any corrections that should be incorporated in future reprints or editions of this book.

A Cataloguing-in-Publication entry is available from the National Library of Australia, www.nla.gov.au

Contents

Introduction	1
What is Catholic Identity?	3
Jesus	8
Frontier	12
Liturgy and Prayer	16
Curriculum	20
Pedagogy	25
Staff Formation	30
Ecological Conversion	34
Family, Parish and School	37
Charity and Justice	40
Befriending Difference	46
Data and Planning	49
Doing Theology	53

Acknowledgements

I am deeply indebted to my colleagues in Catholic Education in South Australia who have shown me what Catholic identity looks like when it is a cogent, contemporary and vibrant reality in our schools. There are too many of you to name individually, such has been the diversity and quantity of your many contributions. There are obvious ways in which the Catholic identity of our schools needs to improve, but our desire for the very best should not blind us to the quality and value of what we already have.

I begin by expressing my appreciation to the principals and assistant principals (Religious Identity and Mission) who have welcomed me into their schools. A special thank you to the teachers who opened up their classrooms; each of you has cause to feel proud of what you are achieving with your students.

Similarly, I am grateful for the rich contributions made by colleagues in schools and the Catholic Education Office who read drafts and suggested activities for the book. Your photographs and suggestions have been invaluable, as has been your ongoing encouragement. Those of you who are members of our Leuven network will surely recognise threads of conversations and insights that have emerged in that life-giving forum. I hope that those of you who have given of your particular expertise in areas such as theological method can see your work reflected in mine. A special debt of gratitude is owed to Professor Didier Polleyfeyt and Jan Bouwens, whose scholarship is referenced throughout the text.

A number of you have walked very closely with me at each step along the way with this book and I couldn't have written it without you. You know who you are, and I am the better for having worked with you. Of course the students whose work and images have been included lie at the heart of this project's purpose.

To Jim and Therese D'Orsa, I express my gratitude for the wisdom and commitment you have demonstrated throughout the project. I hope the book bears the imprint of the bishops and other diocesan colleagues who have opened up a vision of what Church is and can become. I take full responsibility, however, for any inadequacies in my rendering. Finally, to my family I say thank you for showing me what Catholic identity can and can't be in our time. I also hope I haven't been grumpy too often as this book has been largely written out of hours. Your graciousness is a blessing.

I trust the flecks of Catholic gold that are found throughout Catholic schools in South Australia are obvious to the reader. If I may be permitted to change metaphors, I hope this text helps you to appreciate deeply the seeds of possibility that are continually germinating in your own school. May these seeds grow and flourish in your midst.

Introduction

Do you believe Catholic schools can proclaim the Gospel uniquely and powerfully in our nation? If you do, this book is written for you. If you are a principal, a staff member, a parent, a parish leader or someone in the community who believes in the potential of Catholic education, this book seeks to explore that potential from a number of vantage points. The religious identity question that has become critical for Catholic schools is a key driver for the book.

The Catholic school is an educational community where learning, culture, faith and life find a meeting place. The challenge of making this meeting place meaningful for students lies at the heart of the identity challenge faced by Catholic schools in our time. It is a challenge that is invigorating but demanding and becoming more sophisticated as each year unfolds.

Sometimes the approach taken in explorations of Catholic identity is to define 'Catholic' by referring to abstract principles or concepts. The phrase 'Catholic is as Catholic does' sums up the approach taken in this book. Instead of considering identity issues purely from a theoretical perspective, the book draws from living examples of school life. I am indebted here to Catholic Education in South Australia because this rich community of schools has provided the Catholic ferment out of which this book has matured. A picture of contemporary Catholic identity is built up, layer upon layer, over the chapters of the book, each of which focuses on a particular facet of the Catholic school. There are chapters which explore Catholic identity from vantage points as diverse as pastoral care, curriculum and pedagogy, disability, prayer and ecological sustainability.

Pope Francis has captured the imagination of Catholics and the wider international community with the warmth of his personality and the accessibility of his humanity. In his recent Apostolic Exhortation, Francis stated that he wanted a Church that 'is bruised, hurting and dirty because it has been out on the streets, rather than a Church which is unhealthy from being confined and from clinging to its own security' (Evangelii Gaudium, # 49). Francis' statement is very relevant for Catholic schools, and the fragments of school life presented in this book are offered as examples of the mission to be 'out on the streets' meeting the needs of the families and the children who have been entrusted to us. Faithfulness to this mission is the surest guide to constructing an authentic Catholic identity in our time.

While the operating environment for Catholic schools presents a myriad of challenges for those who lead them, it also presents a myriad of opportunities. This book seeks to share in the vigour and hope expressed by Francis when he acknowledged that every period presents its particular obstacles to the proclamation of the Gospel – 'we know that the Roman Empire was not conducive to the Gospel message, the struggle for justice, or the defence of human dignity. Every period of history is marked by the presence of human weakness, self-absorption, complacency and selfishness' (Evangelii Gaudium, # 263).

I have written this book on the premise that Catholic schools already provide a living witness to the Gospel, but there is nothing about their religious identity that can be taken for granted. Many of our staff, students and families will only experience the tradition as being meaningful if they are invited to make new points of connection with Catholic faith. If they are reconnected in this way, they will see themselves as part of the ongoing story as the tradition evolves from one generation to the next. Each era opens up new chapters that enhance and develop the tradition. Seeing yourself and your school as part of the story is central to being authentically Catholic.

Our schools fulfil their mission when those who lead them embrace the threads of faith, hope and love that are woven from the stories of school life such as those presented in this book. Pope Francis called us to 'try a little harder to take the first step and to become involved' (Evangelii Gaudium, # 24). Everyone who leads a Catholic school has already taken many first steps and is deeply involved. There is, however, always another challenge that emerges when it comes to responding to the ongoing call of the Gospel. I hope the experience of reading this book opens up a challenge and a call to you as you engage with the examples and reflections in the text.

Although an academic approach to Catholic identity is not taken in this book, it does rest upon a firm foundation of research. Catholic cultural anthropologist Gerry Arbuckle's work has reinforced the conviction that story and narrative provide the basic building blocks for any person or group's identity (Arbuckle, 2013). Paul Ricoeur's hermeneutic philosophy has also highlighted the ways in which narratives, symbols and metaphors shape and animate the identity formation process (Ricoeur, 1995). Catholic schools have a strong religious identity when those who belong to them draw sensitively from the treasures of the Catholic faith to create rich and formative spaces for their students.

Missiologists Jim and Therese D'Orsa make the case for us being in a 'liminal age' in their books published earlier in this Mission and Education series. Liminal experiences can occur at the personal or cultural level. For example, at the time of writing this text, my family is packing up our home in preparation for an interstate move. We are in a time of personal liminality as we move out of valued relationships and dismantle our home. Of course we will find a new home and build a new network of employment and social relationships, but we are 'in the middle' – in a frontier space – with our old home going and our new home not yet found. It is disturbing and challenging to be in a liminal space, and some of these challenges are discussed further in the chapter on Frontier. Members of cultures in liminal times can feel disturbed and unsure as many taken-for-granted assumptions are called into question in areas such as family, Church, and the wider world (D'Orsa & D'Orsa, 2013). This liminality is the result of extraordinary changes caused by globalisation and its attendant phenomena such as the pluralisation of society. It is also caused by the near collapse of the tight Catholic culture we Catholics experienced until recently in Australia. Catholic schools need strong and visionary leadership in this liminal age if their communities are to 'make meaning' in a time when basic assumptions about life are changing. This book will join with Jim and Therese in their conclusion that school leaders can only make meaning in a Catholic context when they are able to 'do theology' with and in their school communities.

The examples of school life that are presented in this book were chosen because they are typical of the efforts being made by educators to provide their students with meaningful points of encounter with elements of our faith tradition. Canadian philosopher Charles Taylor has characterised our age as being shaped by an 'ethic of authenticity' where each individual must discover the point of their life themselves, rather than conforming to a model imposed externally from society or some religious or political authority (Taylor, 1991). Sociologist Philip Hughes found, in his report on a very significant study of the spirituality of young people in Australia, that young people 'put life together' themselves rather than following a predetermined way given to them by others (Hughes, 2007). In his reflections on Taylor's thought, James McEvoy points out that individuals only understand themselves through significant relationships and in the context of the communities to which they belong (McEvoy, 2009). Catholic schools are seen in these reflections as providing students with a community where they can make sense of their lives by engaging with rich and contemporary Catholic beliefs, values and practices.

The Catholic University of Leuven in Belgium has worked closely with the Catholic Education Commission of Victoria to research the religious identity options being taken up in Catholic schools (Pollefeyt & Bouwens, 2010). It is clear from this research that students will only commit to beliefs when they have played an active role in understanding them. The Leuven research provides powerful insights for school leaders who wish to understand the religious identity options being exercised within their communities and the implications of those options for the mission of the school.

I invite you to join with me in reflecting on the Catholic identity of your community by engaging with the examples of school life presented in this book as well as the research that is woven in and around the examples, providing a theoretical framework for the narrative.

What is Catholic Identity?

If you were to draw a diagram of the Catholic identity of your school, would you come up with something like the one I have developed below? I have been intrigued by the responses to the diagram in the workshops where I have used it. For example, one colleague said that her school always places the student at the centre of their thinking, and yet in this diagram I have replaced the student with God. This comment led to a deep conversation about the relationship between Catholic identity, God and the students.

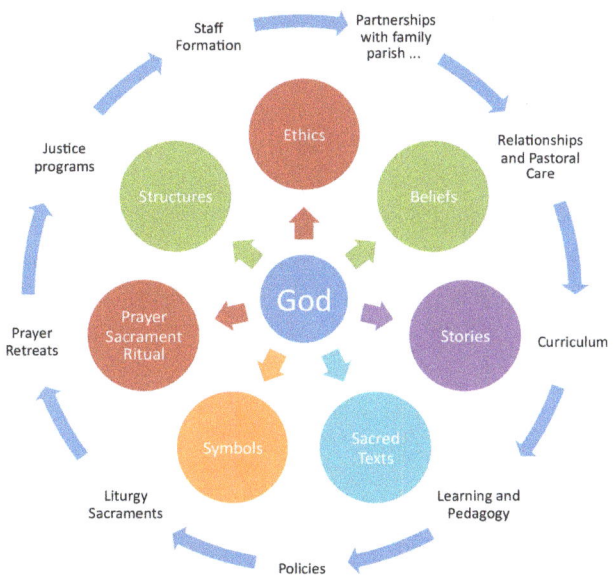

Draw your own diagram

▲ Reflect on your experiences of your school. What is it about your story that seems significant?

▲ Consider how you could represent something from your story on a diagram or an image.

▲ Consider the differences between your diagram and the one above.

▲ Should God be at the centre of the diagram or should the student? Or is there a way in which this dilemma can be resolved by making them both central in some way?

Reflection and action are essential

We will reflect further on the diagram as this chapter unfolds, but before going there I wanted to reflect on a bushwalk I recently experienced. I had been out with my wife walking in a very scenic part of the Mount Lofty Ranges when we came across a friend by chance and we began to walk with him. Our friend stopped periodically to show us the orchids that up until then we had been walking past without noticing. The intricacy and beauty of the world that we had been walking through without being aware of it was amazing once it was pointed out to us. Seeing and understanding what is happening in a Catholic school's identity can be a bit like that. You can walk around the school without noticing very much or you can attend to what is happening and take active steps to amplify religious opportunities and moments as they continually arise in the busy life that surrounds you.

It is a wonderful thing to behold the skill and sensitivity of leaders who have mastered the art of religious leadership. These leaders see Catholic faith as a treasure box filled with riches that students and staff can draw upon continuously in the life of the school. Skilled religious leaders know how to create an environment where staff and students draw deeply from the tradition to provide new points of access and meaning for the communities they lead.

God has been placed at the centre of my Catholic identity diagram because everything that happens in a Catholic school should draw its deepest meaning from God. While this is an easy sentence to write, putting it into practice in the life of the school is both sophisticated and challenging. Various elements of religious traditions are represented inside the diagram: Scriptures, sacraments, stories, symbols and beliefs. The religious identity of a Catholic school is built up daily by drawing effectively and sensitively from these elements as opportunities arise in the life of the school. The outer rim of the diagram represents typical opportunities for religious formation in a Catholic school. Moments in school life such as retreats, pastoral care, relationships, liturgy and the promotion of justice provide opportunities for the school community to experience Catholic faith as a living and meaningful reality in their lives.

activity

This activity is designed for a gathering of members of the school community, such as a staff meeting, a board meeting or a Religious Education classroom.

The image of God that people have in the school community powerfully shapes the school's Catholic identity. Gather a range of photos, writing, symbols, images, books, statues, etc., and ask people to pick one that they most identify with and then explain that affinity to a colleague, slowly bringing the sharing to a whole staff interaction. What commonalities and differences are there in the way in which staff perceive God?

While the outer rim of the diagram above defines what Catholic schools do, this activity only becomes authentic when the inner elements are seen as real, connected and important. Doing and being have to be held together and integrated in the life of a Catholic school. Reflection and action are both integral to the religious leadership that needs to be exercised continuously at all levels within the school community.

Religious leadership is storytelling

As was mentioned in the introduction, we are living in a 'liminal age' where many taken-for-granted assumptions from the past about family, culture and Church are being contested. The challenge that leaders of Catholic schools face in this liminal age is to help their communities 'make meaning' in a time when basic assumptions about life are changing.

Gerry Arbuckle is a Catholic priest whose anthropological insights help me to understand what effective religious leadership looks like in our liminal times. Arbuckle highlights the importance of storytelling in the process of identity formation for both individuals and institutions, and he says that this storytelling becomes particularly important in times of change when traditional meaning systems are breaking down and new ones need to be created.

Those who lead Catholic schools are storytellers who draw from the deep wells of Catholic faith to open up a narrative with their communities that is meaningful and life-giving given the local context and culture of the school. The school's Catholic narrative is developed from elements such as those represented in the inside circle of the diagram above: Scriptures, sacraments, stories, symbols and beliefs. For Catholics, God is mediated richly and deeply in such elements as they are experienced in an ecclesial community like a Catholic school. Effective religious leaders know how to weave these elements together into a story that makes sense to people and leads them into faith experiences that are meaningful and relevant for their lives.

In his analysis of Catholic identity, Arbuckle (2013) distinguished between myths and narrative. Myths are the deep founding stories handed down to us from the past that explain how the world is and how we relate ourselves to that world and all of the people in it. Those who study Scripture and Theology tap into the deep wells (or myths) of Catholic faith in a particularly explicit way. While myths are past stories, narratives are told by people in the present. Narratives create identity in the here and now by drawing on myths from the past and retelling them within the changing times of the present. Catholic liturgy can be understood as the source and summit of our faith because of the way in which it makes the ancient myths present to us in a particularly real and cogent way. Every religious leader needs to open up a narrative that is built up from elements of the tradition such as those represented inside the diagram at the start of this chapter. While the deep myths and beliefs from our Catholic faith are unchanging throughout history, each community needs to develop its own narrative from those deep beliefs in ways that make sense, given the local context and culture. Religious symbols, liturgy, pastoral practice, Scripture and Catholic teaching all cohere into a meaning-filled narrative when skilled religious leadership is exercised.

reflection

▲ Can your religious leadership be understood as a story that you are sharing with your community as you weave Catholic elements together into a narrative that makes sense to your community?

▲ What are some of the features of the religious story that your community is telling itself and others?

▲ How effectively do you draw from the deep meaning structures (myths) of Catholic faith in the stories that you are telling with your community members today?

▲ Whose voices are not being heard in the Catholic story unfolding in your school?

Identity – stable and changing

There are many ways to understand the meaning of the word 'identity'. If you look in a dictionary you are likely to find something like 'the set of characteristics by which a person, group or thing is recognised'. I find it helpful to draw from the reflections of French philosopher Paul Ricoeur as I explore what identity means for a school. Ricoeur considered how identities are both stable and changing at the same time.

An individual or a group needs to have a stable set of characteristics if they are going to have an identity that is recognisable from one day to the next. If an individual looked one way today and completely different tomorrow then they would be unrecognisable – they would have no identity. So one thing we can say about personal identity is that it relies upon a set of stable features that can be recognised by those who know us. This is true not only of our physical characteristics but also of our character, our personality and our worldview.

If you were to describe someone you know, you would probably refer to the physical attributes or personality traits that stand out for you in that person. However, our identity is never fully captured by saying we have brown hair or a good sense of humour. A person or a group's identity is built up in many complex layers that cannot be reduced to a few simple labels.

The late Bishop Michael Putney gave a keynote address to a Conference where he counselled against defining Catholic identity too narrowly, using one's own experience as a yardstick or using one or other element as the defining feature of what it means to be Catholic. Catholic identity cannot be reduced to a series of dot points or simple slogans. The Catholic tradition of faith has grown over millions of lifetimes spanning a myriad of times, places and cultures. Paradoxically though, while recognising that Catholic identity is always larger than its local expressions, Catholic faith always and ultimately has to be lived as a commitment in the mind, heart and hands of each Catholic person, formed in a Catholic community that is located in a particular point in time and culture.

Changing identities

While identities are stable, they are not fixed. Change and maturation over time is inevitable. I heard my niece saying recently that it is 'lame' being 12 and that 13 is not a much better age in her view. She was looking forward to being 14. I hope she isn't disappointed. Sometimes those of us who are a little older than 14 can yearn for the physical attributes we had in earlier years, but time marches on nonetheless and we can either befriend what is happening to us or we can rail against the way we are.

Just as individuals have an identity that grows and develops, so too do groups. Groups survive by adapting to changes in their environments. Groups and institutions that fail to move with the times run the risk of becoming irrelevant or outmoded. Those who focus and strengthen a Catholic school's religious identity must move with the social and cultural currents of their time, even as they draw deeply from the ancient wells of the Tradition. Arbuckle points out that every group has a culture which 'tells' people how they should feel, think and act. As has been noted, this group culture has its roots in myths that are narrated in an ongoing way according to present context and culture. Culture provides people with an essential sense of purpose, order and belonging. In times of cultural change, members of the group easily

feel that they are in chaos and in danger of losing their identities. One of the challenges of leadership at such times is to lead people through the chaos and out the other side by drawing deeply from the cultural myths to tell new stories that make sense in the new times.

reflection

▲ Change is challenging. Is there an example in your community where you are holding on to what is authentic and meaningful even as you develop new expressions that open Catholic faith out with new points of connection and access?

What makes us Catholic?

Brainstorm with staff a variety of ways that your school demonstrates its Catholic identity. When this is done, ask the staff to identify from their brainstorm all the qualities, actions, values, etc., that would look equally at home in the brainstorm of the local state school down the road. Stress with staff that what they have chosen could well be examples of Catholic identity but may need to be more explicitly engaged with the tradition so that the Catholic dimension is foregrounded.

Ask whether there were items identified for the Catholic school that could not be easily part of a secular state school identity. What were these? Do these elements lead you to the heart of your school's Catholic identity?

Are there other elements of your identity list which are important but need further reflection before their connections with the tradition are apparent?

CASE STUDY

RELIGIOUS LEADERSHIP
Putting the Vision Statement to Work

A large metal banner hangs prominently above the front desks in the very busy reception area of the school. The words engraved on the banner express the school's mission statement:

'A spirit centred community of learners inspired by Jesus seeking integrity and fullness of life.'

Teachers explore the meaning of the Vision Statement with their students, and board members use the statement as a guide for their work. At all times the message is: How can we live this vision through our work and relationships in the school?

The principal says that the process of developing the school's Vision Statement made a very significant contribution to the Catholic identity of her school. Each word was considered very carefully, but the principal feels that the process of developing the statement was even more important than the end product of the statement itself. The participation of staff, students and their families over an extended time in creating the statement meant that the community owned and appropriated its meaning in a much more significant way.

A Building Opening

The opening of a new school building can unfold as a perfunctory event to thank those involved in the building's creation or to acknowledge those who paid for it. I was struck recently by one school whose leaders view each new school building as giving the community a new sense of itself – a new identity. Buildings are seen in the school as signs of God's grace, and each opening becomes an opportunity to express the school's religious identity through blessings and prayers, thanks and praise, word and procession.

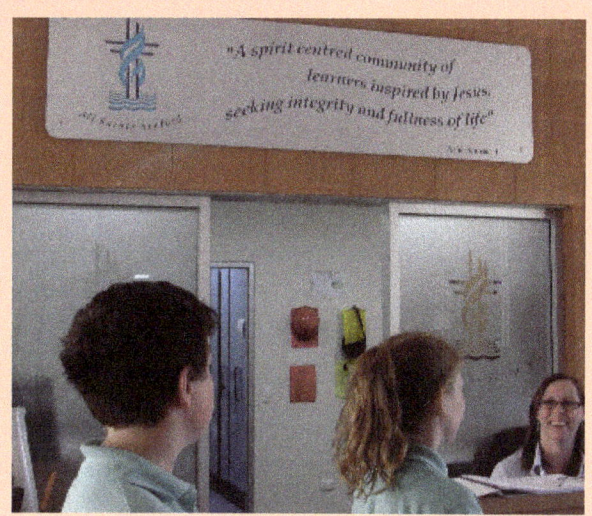

The opening was clearly grounded in the Catholic identity of the school, even as it expressed the vibrant cultural and religious diversity of the school community. As the guests entered the building, they were greeted by students and staff in traditional cultural dress, and during the liturgy, prayers were offered up in Maltese, Vietnamese, Chinese, Italian, Hazaragi and Spanish. Afterwards we were shown hospitality through the food and dance of many cultures and religions.

Those of us who attended the opening were surrounded by Catholic threads that were carefully woven throughout the celebration. This was a Catholic ceremony rich in image and text, ritual and wonder. The Catholic Book of Blessings gave the ceremony its shape and form, and the homily and prayers clearly placed Christ's love at the centre of the educational enterprise. The opening of the building became a deep expression of the school's cultural diversity grounded in Catholic faith.

Jesus

The image above was created from the work of a young student in one of our schools. I like the fact that the text is not easy to read because it reminds me that many students find our Catholic beliefs hard to 'read' and understand. For those of you who are like me and don't come from a Junior Primary background, the text reads as follows: *Then the people that wanted to save Jesus tried to get him back. But Jesus said 'the soldiers are coming. Just go now that's an order'. 'Yes Jesus' so they goed.*

This text is an extract from an eight page bible that a student wrote at his own initiative for his Religious Education coordinator. I think texts like these go to the heart of the mission of the Catholic school. As I read the Gospels, one of the most confronting questions Jesus asks is, 'Who do you say that I am?'

The Jesus KPI

If God is at the centre of the Catholic school, then the response that students have to this question of Jesus – Who do you say I am? – becomes a key performance indicator for the school. This is so because Christians believe God really became one of us in Jesus. Christian faith is planted in the soil of history and students in a Catholic school must learn about the life and times of Jesus as a person. Equally importantly they must be exposed to the mystery of the incarnation and the radical belief that God is truly human in Jesus. Christian faith means appreciating that Jesus was not only a historical character but also someone who is truly present across history in the midst of the believing community. The Gospel calls us into the mystery of Christ, who is continually present to us, inviting us to 'build the Kingdom of God' with him.

This mystery is profound and bears a lifetime of fathoming in faith. While Catholic schools can only accompany students for a fraction of their faith pilgrimage, they shoulder a unique privilege and responsibility nonetheless to build the Kingdom of God within the school community. The Kingdom or Reign of God that Jesus proclaimed in the Gospel is built whenever God's grace is present in loving relationships, whenever truth and freedom are promoted and whenever healing, social justice, ecological harmony and peace are fostered in our world.

While some of our students come to school with very deep faith backgrounds in the family, in many cases they do not. If the school is to educate the students,

Jesus and the students

▲ Identify a moment in your professional practice, recent or past, when you thought that a student or students were in a Jesus moment. Write a brief story about this moment.

▲ Share your story with one other person. Circle the verbs in your story that tell you what the students were doing and what they were saying. What makes this a Jesus moment?

▲ Develop an image that conveys something significant about the moment that you have identified.

▲ Create a display of the images that have been created. What is the potential of this exhibit for coming to a shared understanding of Jesus? How do you see Jesus' mission and message in these images? What are the implications for teaching and learning?

---

then the starting place is where they are, not some other imaginary place. I am amazed at how teachers are able to introduce students to key Christian concepts and ideas, even within a relatively short time at school.

I know that the KPI proposal I made above raises complex issues. The answer that students give to the question of Jesus, 'Who do you say that I am?', can only fully be given from a Christian perspective as a result of the gift of faith, not as an outcome of a well-delivered curriculum. Schools cannot presume to give to students what belongs to God, but they can take responsibility for the quality and substance of the 'Jesus spaces' and 'kingdom spaces' they create.

reflection

▲ What answer would your students give to the question, 'Who do you say that I am?'

▲ Do you agree with the idea of making the answer to this question a key performance indicator for the Catholic school?

▲ Do you consciously try to build up a sense of God's Kingdom or Reign in the life of the school? How would you describe what this looks like to others?

Switching the students on to Jesus

At a recent conference, Didier Pollefeyt, the promoter of the Belgian research being referred to throughout this book, recounted the story of the student, the teacher and the squirrel. The teacher began the Religious Education lesson by indicating that the class would be learning about a squirrel. One of the students put up her hand and said, 'We don't want to hear the story of the squirrel'. When the teacher asked, 'Why?' the student said, 'Because we all know that by the end of the class the squirrel will be Jesus'. While the audience laughed, they also knew that there was an important pedagogical point being made. Sometimes the way Jesus is presented in the curriculum can become predictable for students, and they switch off.

Engaging students in their learning is one of the hallmarks of successful teaching. Knowing who the students are, what interests them, what connects them with the subject matter, what prior knowledge is being built upon and mastering a range of strategies that open up rich learning experiences are all elements of successful teaching. Sometimes the simplest strategies can be the most effective. One teacher I know asks her students at the start of the year to write down what they wonder about in the religion area and what they want to know or understand. She invites them to describe Jesus to someone who had no idea and to write something about their image of God. This information provides a basis for the way she structures the curriculum during the year.

The formal Religious Education curriculum opens up an explicit space for learning about Jesus, and it is obvious to any teacher when the students have become caught up in their learning. I can remember a Year 12 class where we were studying the Acts of the Apostles and a student raised his hand to observe that the Church is still wrestling with some of the issues that were an issue for the community being described in Acts. It was a magical moment.

This 'learning about' Jesus must, however, be complemented with 'experiences of' Jesus in the midst of the ecclesial community that is the Catholic school. The broader religious life of the school has the potential to offer many rich opportunities for encountering Jesus, who is present in prayer and liturgy, present in positive pastoral care, present in the school's concern for the poor and present in the challenges to care more deeply for God's creation and our part in it.

Jesus is not just a good man

Later in this book, reference will be made to the Leuven research that challenges 'reductionist' and 'restorationist' religious identity options. A reductionist approach to Jesus portrays him in terms of values such as caring and forgiving. The problem with such an approach is that it reduces Jesus to a 'good man', rather than leading students to grapple with fundamental Christian mysteries such as the significance of the incarnation and Jesus' resurrection. A school's Catholic identity is hollowed out over time into a shell of itself when this approach is taken. The restorationist approach, on the other hand, asks students to accept Catholic beliefs without giving them the opportunity to interpret the doctrines or understand them in the context of contemporary culture with all its many alternatives for making meaning. This approach often results in students rejecting religious commitment because they have not been able to engage in the processes by which they can appropriate the meaning of Catholic doctrines into their own lives.

The research referred to throughout this book indicates that students will only find a belief meaningful and worthy of their commitment *if they have had the opportunity to actively make sense of it* themselves. With this in mind, students must continually be invited into experiences which challenge them to make sense of the faith tradition, not only by engaging with it explicitly, but also by engaging with it in ways that *connect deeply with what matters most in their lives*.

Teachers who understand that it is neither possible nor appropriate to impose beliefs on students will instinctively avoid strategies which are restorationist and will attempt to introduce students to a Catholic understanding of Jesus by finding ways to connect the Church's understanding of who Jesus is with what matters most in the students' lives. On the other hand, following the reductionist path of reducing the message and mission of Jesus to abstract 'Gospel values' robs students of the opportunity to encounter the mystery of the person who is proclaimed in the Gospel. Values such as 'friendship' or 'forgiveness' need to be presented in ways that amplify the person, message and mission of Jesus rather than reducing him to being 'a good man'.

Christians believe in a God who is a Trinity of persons, a God who created the universe in love, who truly became human in Jesus and who suffered and died for us and rose from the dead, just as we too find new life as we die to ourselves and live anew in Christ. Catholics understand these beliefs in the context of their ongoing participation in the liturgy, sacraments, charity, social action, ecological conversion and the wider teaching of their Church. We believe that our lives are animated by the Spirit who dwells within us as we live in a world filled with grace. Christian mysteries such as these are not easy to explore with students, but it is essential that they are opened up nonetheless. Knowledge, skill and collegial support are required if the curriculum and the broader religious life of the school is to invite students into the depth of what is offered to them in Catholic faith.

While the religious dimension of curriculum in a Catholic school has a strong cognitive dimension, Christian faith is not reduced to cognition. Christian faith is 'not the result of an ethical choice or a lofty idea, but the encounter with an event, a person, which gives life a new horizon and a decisive direction' (Benedict XVI, 2005, # 1). Catholic schools have the deep privilege and the clear responsibility to play their part in introducing students to the mystery and significance of Jesus for the students who have been entrusted to their care.

The Jesus of the Gospel comes with a mission, a message and an ethos that Catholic schools must communicate. This is an essential part of what they do as 'Catholic'. They also provide a context in which the Kingdom of God, central to Jesus' mission and message, is lived out in practice. That is, the local Catholic school provides an increasingly important 'plausibility structure' for religious commitment in an era when other structures tend to be breaking down. In this context, religious leadership means that schools explicitly make connections between Jesus, Kingdom and the daily life of the school.

reflection

▲ Do members of your school community see Jesus as being anything more than just a good man?

Our community's image of Jesus

The following activity can be undertaken in a staff meeting, at a school board or with a group of parents or students. It can unfold within a single session or developed into a more comprehensive process within your school community.

- Begin by asking how your school community communicates the mission and the message of Jesus of the Gospel.

- What are some of the places where this message might be made visible to the community? For example, the school website or a permanent exhibit.

- What image of a Jesus moment might the students bring from their daily lives? Allow yourself to wonder why this is a Jesus moment for them …

- What image of a Jesus moment might the families bring from their daily lives? Discuss why this is a Jesus moment for them.

- Reflect for a moment on Jesus moments in scripture and ask yourself which of these moments have the greatest relevance to the children and why.

- Consider how the community could discern these moments to see what they have to say about the deepest desires and yearnings of community members.

- Reflect together on the ways in which the mission and message of Jesus of the Gospel might be communicated more clearly and strongly in your community.

Frontier

Do you hear expressions like 'churched' or 'unchurched' used in your school community? I feel these expressions take us into the wrong space when it comes to reflecting on the Catholic identity of the school.

Working in a frontier space

A most evocative way to think about Catholic schools is to see them as 'frontiers'. The picture below shows a section of Hadrian's Wall, a 118 km long border built in the second century on the northern frontier of the Roman Empire. I always enjoy having a few people of Scottish descent in the audience when I point out that this wall represented the line between civilisation and barbarians – the Scots in the group are quick to share their views on which side of the wall the barbarians lived!

Jacques Haers, a theologian at the Catholic University of Leuven, speaks beautifully and evocatively of what it is to be on the frontier. He says that one way is to see the frontier as a dividing line between 'us' and 'them'. The expressions civilised/barbarian or churched/unchurched are examples of this us/them attitude. I see this polarised attitude as sitting within a 'separation paradigm' where the border is a way of keeping different people separate from each other. Another way to appreciate frontiers is to think of them as thickened lines where people encounter each other.

The word 'frontier' comes from *frons* – the Latin word for face. With this in mind, a frontier can become a space where people 'encounter one another on a territory that is only partially familiar, that contains unfamiliar and as yet unmapped, unexpected features' (Haers, 2004).

When someone works within the separation paradigm, the frontier is a place where territory is invaded and the borderline guarded so that people are only admitted over to the other side when they meet certain criteria. When people work within a paradigm of *encounter*, the borderline thickens and opens up so that people face each other and create new and shared meanings together. We have seen earlier in the chapter on Catholic identity that any person or group must always have some defining characteristics if they are to have an identity. One of the challenges for those who lead Catholic schools is to ensure that the defining characteristics of the school's religious identity are respected, preserved and nurtured. In this sense, leaders have to know and respect the 'boundaries' of Catholic faith that provide the framework for their work in the frontier.

As well as respecting the boundaries of Catholic faith, school leaders also need to ensure that new forms and expressions are continually being created so that the school's religious identity is experienced as meaningful and living within the diverse contexts and cultures of the students, staff and families. In this sense, school leaders are always working in a frontier space – in territory that is both strange and familiar at the same time. In this frontier space, religious leaders tell a religious story with their community members that is ever-old and ever-new.

It takes courage to work in the frontier space because, by definition, the territory is unknown and you never know what might emerge 'from the other side'. Ancient Roman and Mediaeval map makers sometimes used to mark the edges of the map with a phrase like *hic sunt dracones* (here be dragons) and included a drawing of a dragon or some other dangerous creature just to underscore the dangers inherent in moving beyond the settled territory into the unknown. Notwithstanding the dangers, those who lead Catholic schools need to find the courage to work at the frontiers their schools present as they 'face' their community members and open up new points of connection between the ancient Catholic faith and the ever-new contexts and cultures in which it is appropriated. Later in this book we will explore the concept of 'doing theology' and argue that leaders need to work closely with their colleagues to do theology and develop new expressions of the faith that are authentically Catholic as well as being culturally resonant.

reflection

▲ What are the frontier spaces in your school? How can they become thickened spaces where people face and encounter each other more richly and deeply?

▲ How do people encounter and befriend difference in your school?

▲ What boundaries need to be respected and what boundaries need to be overcome in your school?

CASE STUDY

Catholic School as 'Frontier Space'

These butterflies located on a cross are the outcome of a rich engagement in a frontier space. The Leadership Team of the school worked with a metal sculptor and a number of parents who had been identified as not being strongly engaged with the school. The parents were invited to a wine and cheese evening to share their stories and reasons for low school engagement. They were invited to say what Catholic identity they were seeking for their daughters from the school.

Over a series of meetings the parents walked around the school and discussed the symbols they saw and what might be created as an expression of the school's Catholic identity. They workshopped their ideas with a sculptor and the Leadership Team, who reflected with the group on various passages of Scripture. The process culminated in the production of a cross adorned with three butterflies which represented the hope that comes from the resurrection of Jesus, the love that God pours out on us all and the emergence into adulthood that is such a feature of life in this girls' middle school.

Another example of life in the frontier space is the principal who decided to move outside the gate at the end of the school day to talk with the parents who stayed on the street side of the fence rather than coming into the school to pick up their children as most parents did. He asked them what could be done differently in the community to help them to feel more welcome in the school.

The frontier space is not just populated by 'marginal people' who don't quite fit in to the mainstream of the school, although these people can take us into the frontier in a particularly effective way. Everyone is called to be at the frontier. None of us has all of the answers, and each of us can be touched by the grace that becomes obvious to us when we reflect on what is happening in the busy flow of relationships, insights, conflicts and challenges that permeate the life of a school.

Our faith is ever-old and ever-new, and it is born again in a frontier space when people face each other and discover the mystery of Christ opening up in their midst. This mystery might unfold in a caring act, in a liturgy or in any space where we step outside the comfort of what is familiar to us and discover how God might be present to us in ways that we had neither expected nor imagined. Schools are particularly rich places, filled with busy relationships, events, failures, successes, hopes and anxieties. Those of us who are able to work in frontier spaces can help each other to discover God in our midst, at the centre of our experience and richly in the midst of busy school life.

Life on the frontier

Catholic schools are portrayed in this chapter as operating in a frontier space where people encounter each other so that what was strange becomes familiar. This is a process of 'befriending' and overcoming alienation.

- ▲ Where and when do you experience a space of encounter in your school?
- ▲ Who is included?
- ▲ Where and when do you experience a space of disconnection in your school?
- ▲ Who is excluded?

Where are the dragons in your school and how do you befriend them, even as you allow them to challenge you?

Liturgy and Prayer

If God is at the centre of the Catholic school, then prayer and liturgy play a unique and critical role in the formation of the school's Catholic identity. God can hardly be at the centre of the school if staff and students do not spend time with God in prayer.

I recently visited a Reception/Year 1 class and had a wonderful experience of their morning prayer. The children moved easily and naturally into their routine: one child laid out a prayer mat and the children sat around it. One student lit a candle and a number of other students placed angel figurines that they had made around the candle. The prayer was sacred and intimate, and we prayed together for issues and concerns that ranged from pets through to world peace. The innocence and beauty of the prayer was palpable. I found myself wondering how many thousands of classrooms were praying at this depth around the nation.

I was talking with a colleague who had led a Year 12 retreat program for a number of years and she described a beautiful ceremony that was the highlight of the retreat each year for the students. Towards the end of the retreat, students gathered in a circle around a candle and the leader spoke to them about Christ being the light of the world, the light that shines in each one of us. Students and their teachers were asked to spend some time in silence reflecting on their friends and peers in the room and the ways in which they have shown the light of Christ to them. Students were then invited to take the candle and give it to a student or a teacher, naming the light that the person had given to them. Often the person giving the candle would hold it for a period of time while the person was receiving it and they would have their hands together on the candle representing Christ. The ceremony was always a deeply spiritual experience and highlight for the retreat. The students by Year 12 had the maturity and respect to understand how to enter into the experience and no one was ever left out, with staff and students all being incorporated, including students on the margins or with special needs.

There are many ways of praying, and our Christian tradition is laden with treasures that may be called up by educators to create formative spaces for the students so that they can experience different types of prayer and have the opportunity to discover what works for them. In this chapter we will explore two prayer forms that the Australian Catholic bishops promoted during the recent Year of Grace – the Examen and Lectio Divina. Both of these prayer forms have deep roots in the tradition and are used in our schools.

The Examen is a way of praying that was developed by Saint Ignatius of Loyola, and the version promoted in the Year of Grace began with questions such as: What am I most thankful for today? and, When was I most able to give and receive love today? The Examen then moves into questions such as: What has troubled me today? and, When was I least able to give and receive love? The concluding moments of the Examen are shaped by the questions: How have I met Jesus today? and, What am I being invited to do?

A Jesuit school that I am familiar with has established the Examen as a major part of its prayer life. They use a form of Examen based on the acronym 'THINK with God'.

> **T**hank you God for …
>
> **H**elp me to understand why …
>
> **I** look at my day/week and …
>
> **N**ext time I will …
>
> **K**eep with me Jesus as I …

Students offer reflections such as the following about their experience of the Examen:

The Examen helps me to think about my life and be grateful for what I have. The purpose of the Examen is to reflect on our week with God and to strengthen our relationship with God. I feel calm when I do the Examen. If I am going through a tough time it sometimes helps me to understand these times better when I think through it slowly.

Lectio Divina is a very ancient prayer practice in the Church, and the version recommended by the bishops begins with an invitation to read Scripture very slowly once or twice, listening for the word or phrase that stands out. The next step is to let that word or phrase sit quietly in your mind and heart and notice what happens. The third step is one of responding to God. The response could be a word, a hope, a resolution or a prayer. Then there is a moment to listen to what the Scripture is asking in the present situation. Lectio Divina concludes with the resolve to act with love.

I am aware that a number of schools in my diocese have used the Lectio, and they have given students prompts such as the following in their times of prayer: What resonates with you? What does God want to say? How does this affect your life? The Examen and Lectio Divina are just two of a multitude of prayer forms that can be drawn from the wells of Catholic faith. The Catholic identity of the school is animated in a unique way by the creativity and commitment of staff who teach their students to pray.

Meaningful prayer

What makes an experience of informal and formal prayer meaningful? Reflect on this question using an 'X-Chart'. (Make an X-Chart by drawing a big X across the whole of an A4 page to divide the page into four sections. Respond to the questions below in each section.)

- ▲ What would you see?
- ▲ What would you hear?
- ▲ What would it feel like to be involved in this experience?
- ▲ What would the attitudes and thinking be of those present?

The X-Chart could be completed from the perspective of different groups within your community (students, parents, staff) and for different types of liturgy.

Liturgy

I was recently at a national meeting of leaders of Catholic education systems and representatives from Catholic higher education institutions. It was an important and fruitful meeting where we talked about some of the identity issues facing our schools and how our higher education partners could help us address those issues. At one point in the meeting one of the higher education representatives stood up and said strongly that the liturgy in Catholic schools was of a very poor standard and was unlikely to be formative for the students who experienced it. The meeting had been proceeding quite politely up until that point and an awkward silence descended upon the group, such that the Chair of the meeting turned to me and to the other presenter to ask us for a response. The other presenter happened to be an archbishop, so when he indicated that I was the responder on this one, I felt called forth!

I found myself saying that because I did not agree with the premise, I could not agree with the rest of the intervention. I acknowledged that while some schools had a very shallow and unsatisfactory liturgical life, there were also many schools that offered their students rich liturgical experiences. I suggested that it would be more profitable to examine what these later schools were getting right than it would be to start with a presumption that the standard was low in every instance.

When I call to mind schools that celebrate liturgies well, it seems clear to me that they have creative and committed staff who know the tradition and draw upon it richly to ensure that liturgical celebrations are authentic and engaging for their community members. These creative leaders work with others in their communities to build their capacity to prepare liturgies that engage students and provide them with life-giving celebrations. Over time, the experiences that staff and students have of good liturgy is itself formative, so that everyone involved learns the shape of the liturgy and is drawn into its inner power.

Of course, not every school has someone in it who knows the liturgical tradition well enough to build liturgical capacity in their community. Catholic schools that find themselves in such a position have only one choice, and that is the choice they make whenever they need to build capacity in an area critical to mission. The choice is to go and obtain the skills and knowledge necessary and ensure they are shared professionally and widely among staff.

The deep mystery of liturgy

When we enter into a liturgical celebration we step into a deep mystery that has many layers to it. Catholics believe that the Holy Spirit makes Christ present in a very real and unique way in liturgical celebrations. In Eucharistic liturgies we believe that Christ is present in the people who are gathered to pray, in the Scriptures that are proclaimed, in the priest who leads the liturgy and in the communion elements of bread and wine. Catholic schools provide a liturgical catechesis for their students when they teach them about the structure and theology of the Mass and when they provide rich experiences of it regularly in the life of the school. What is true of the Mass is also true of the other sacraments, but the Eucharist provides the focus for these reflections because it is the sacrament celebrated most often in our schools.

Unlike informal forms of prayer, Catholics believe that liturgies belong to the Church and that we do not have the freedom to simply take them and bend their shape around to suit our own purposes. Liturgies have a shape and content that belongs to the whole Church, rather than simply being a creation of the individuals who celebrate it at a given point in time. As Catholics we believe that we are joined with others around the world and across time who are in communion with us when we celebrate the liturgy of the Church. We even believe that we are united with the angels in heaven and participate in an eternal liturgy that includes the saints of the old and new testament and the 'great multitude which no one could number from every nation, race, people, and tongue' (Compendium of the Catechism of the Catholic Church, # 234). With this in mind, great care needs to be taken to ensure that the shape and form of the liturgy is respected whenever it is celebrated.

Of course, talk of angels and the eternal heavenly liturgy may seem quite a long way from the experience of liturgies undertaken in the busy-ness of school life with students, many of whom may be unfamiliar with Catholic symbols and rituals. I find the notion of 'frontier' discussed in an earlier chapter helps me to understand what schools are doing as they lead their students into an appreciation for Catholic liturgy. When we enter the liturgical frontier we are stepping out of 'normal time / normal space' into 'sacred time / sacred space'. We are also leading students from their normal patterns of interaction into patterns which may be partially alien to them.

As noted earlier, a frontier is a space where people 'encounter one another on a territory that is only partially familiar, that contains unfamiliar and as yet unmapped, unexpected features'. One of the hallmarks of an authentic Catholic education, it seems to me, is that students befriend a liturgical tradition that is increasingly alien in our culture. Even as far back as 1939 Carl Jung had observed that while the simplest houses in India have an area curtained off to perform the prayer rites, western houses have no place to escape the phone – 'we always must be ready, we have no time, no place'. If this was noticeable to Jung in 1939, how much more is it the case for us today in our online, connected world. Catholic schools teach their students something powerful for life when they lead them into the inner world and when they teach them about sacred times and places.

If students are to develop an appreciation for liturgy, it must be celebrated well in the life of the school. Good liturgy does not happen accidentally – each school needs to build its liturgical capability so that key staff can lead their students and colleagues into deeper liturgical understandings as liturgies are prepared and celebrated. It goes without saying that there is no substitute for a priest with the skills and attitudes that help all involved experience the mystery of Christ truly present in the liturgy.

While it is critical that the form and integrity of the liturgy is respected, it is equally important to encourage

the full and active participation of those gathered to celebrate the liturgy. In a school context, this means that liturgies must employ language, music and symbols that are accessible to the students, who are often only at the earliest stages of catechesis and therefore need considerable support and assistance to appreciate the liturgical forms and participate fully in them.

Liturgy and justice

Liturgies and prayers are sometimes contrasted with other elements of Catholic identity such as the promotion of justice. Pope Benedict made the point in *Deus Caritas Est* that the Eucharist includes the reality of being loved and of loving others in return. With this in mind, Benedict noted that 'a Eucharist that does not pass over to the concrete practice of love is intrinsically fragmented'. Here we see that the elements of Catholic identity interconnect into an organic whole rather than simply being a collection of disconnected parts. Each element only finds its fullest authentic expression alongside and in sympathy with the other elements. Prayer without justice represents an incomplete and distorted Catholic identity, as does pastoral care without faith.

Catholic schools and Sunday Mass

Participation in Sunday Mass has been such a defining feature of Catholic identity that Catholic schools are sometimes criticised because of the declining numbers of students who attend their local parish. This criticism raises many issues for schools, families and parishes to consider. Schools have little capacity to influence what families decide to do on a weekend, and schools are not responsible for the quality of the liturgies that families experience when they attend Mass on Sundays. With these realities in mind, it is not appropriate to hold schools accountable for student attendance at Sunday Mass. What can schools be held to account for in this critical area of Catholic identity?

I was at a diocesan pastoral planning meeting recently where the facilitator (who was from another diocese) lamented the attitude of some school principals who had said to him that Sunday Mass attendance was not their issue and that they did not see a role for the school to encourage students to attend Mass. In my view this attitude represents an abrogation of responsibility and a failure to make an important contribution to the religious formation of students. We have noted the primary responsibility of families and parishes when it comes to Sunday Mass. Notwithstanding this primacy, schools can provide positive experiences of liturgy during school time and they can reinforce the importance of the Eucharist for Catholic identity and practice.

Improving liturgy and prayer in our school

- ▲ Write down some current features of prayer and liturgy in your school.

- ▲ Imagine your 'happy world' for how prayer and liturgy could be in your school. What would prayer and liturgy look like if it were vibrant, meaningful and engaging for your students? Write down the features of this desired or happy world.

- ▲ Identify the positive forces (drivers) that would support your school to move from the current situation towards the desired situation.

- ▲ Identify the negative forces (blockers) that inhibit movement towards the desired state.

- ▲ Identify what you could do to improve this situation. What lies within your sphere of influence? Remember that removing the blockers can often be more effective than increasing the strength of the drivers.

A student was asked to draw something about his experience of Church and he chose to represent Jesus on the cross with the statement 'I'm bored'. Educators whom I have shown it to have been confronted with the challenge it issues not only for Religious Education as a subject in the curriculum but for the religious dimension of the entire curriculum in the school. One definition of curriculum is 'everything that the school controls'. This picture challenges me to consider how the spaces and activities 'controlled' by the Catholic school might be Catholic and at the same time challenging, life-giving and meaningful for the students. We need a curriculum that is worthy of the students and doesn't bore them – or Jesus either!

There are so many levels at which the issue of curriculum might be addressed. For example, as someone who has recently joined the ACARA Board, I have seen in a clearer way how issues relating to curriculum, assessment and reporting play themselves out nationally among educators and in the political realm. Curriculum debates easily become passionate because the deepest hopes we have for ourselves, our children and our nation have the potential to be translated into expectations for the curriculum of our schools. In fact, one of the criticisms that was levelled at the Australian curriculum early in its development was that it failed to include a rationale for the knowledge and skills included in the curriculum, the organisation of that knowledge or the theories of learning that provide a foundation for the curriculum (Reid, 2010). Reid argued that the Australian curriculum should not only take a position in relation to these issues, but it should also be explicit about the purposes of education, as well as the nature of the curriculum that was being developed and the ways in which equity issues would be addressed in that curriculum.

> ## What is Catholic curriculum?
>
> ▲ What are some of the definitions of curriculum that you use in your school?
>
> ▲ How much of your school's curriculum is actually within the control of your school? Are some important elements of curriculum beyond your control?
>
> ▲ How well are the purposes of education and the nature of education specified in your school?
>
> ▲ To what extent do you believe these purposes should be defined by government? What elements of curriculum should be defined nationally for all schools and what elements should be worked out at a local level?

Catholic schools are required by Church law to be at least as outstanding as other schools in their academic standards (*Code of Canon Law*, 806 #2). If outstanding standards are to be achieved, curriculum leaders in Catholic schools will engage with the very best available nationally in curriculum research, debates and frameworks. While Catholic educators must participate actively in the curriculum discourse, they must do so from a 'Catholic place'. What does it mean to engage with curriculum from a Catholic place?

Catholic curriculum and culture

Jim and Therese D'Orsa (2012) considered the implications of globalisation, secularisation and pluralism for the curriculum of the Catholic school. They reflected on the ways in which students construct knowledge and find meaning in their world. Their analysis considered the ideology of modernity and the implications of competing conceptions of postmodernity for curriculum. Those who develop curriculum in a Catholic school need to understand cultural currents such as these and know how to draw effectively from Catholic beliefs and values as the curriculum is designed and delivered.

It is not possible for every teacher to become a cultural philosopher, but it is essential that those who work in Catholic schools engage with culture and consider the opportunities and constraints it presents for realising the mission of the school. Catholic educators can spend a professional lifetime deepening their understanding of Catholic faith, culture and its implications for curriculum. I briefly explore one example here that concerns the status of knowledge and truth. Many cultural issues could have been chosen for the reflections that follow, but I chose this example because it was found to be a significant issue for young people in a recent research project on youth spirituality and religion. Hughes (2007) found that young people tend to see school subjects such as physics, chemistry and even history and geography as being credible because of their empirical foundations, whereas a subject like religion is seen as being subjective or merely a matter of opinion. While subjects such as science can make legitimate truth claims, subjects like religion are seen as merely a matter of personal belief. Those who are responsible for curriculum development in Catholic schools need to understand this cultural dynamic and design the curriculum accordingly.

Naïve understanding, critical engagement and truth

Paul Ricoeur's notion of the second naïveté provides Catholic educators with a useful framework for exploring the important relationships between relativism, fundamentalism, critical engagement, belief and truth. Ricoeur (1970) traced a threefold movement in interpretation: the interpreter begins in the first stage with an initial naïve acceptance of the text's meaning and moves into the second stage by engaging critically with it. The third and final stage (second naïveté) is reached when the interpreter develops a new understanding of the text's truth, even as the limitations of the initial naïve understanding that became evident in the critical engagement phase are acknowledged and accepted.

An example is helpful at this point to understand how Ricoeur's analysis plays out in real life. Many of us were sceptical in the 1980s when the issue of sexual abuse within the Church first began to be raised more strongly in the public forum. Our naïve understanding was that such reprehensible behaviour was unlikely to have occurred except in the rarest of cases. While some Catholics clung to their initial naïve views, others began to engage critically with the issue. We moved into a critical space where our assumptions and understandings were tested by the facts and by research into psychological pathologies such as paedophilia. We also critiqued clerical power and the way it had been exercised in the Church. For some Catholics this betrayal of trust precipitated a break with their Church that may be temporary or permanent. For very understandable reasons, they are unable to move beyond the stage of critique into a post-critical reconnection with the Church.

Other Catholics have moved into a post-critical understanding of the pathologies that can find expression in the Church as they can in any community of human persons. This post-critical place does not represent a return to a 'first naïveté' – the way they saw things originally. It is never possible to go back again to the first naïveté after one has truly entered a critical space. The post-critical understanding is informed by the critique but is not defined by it. Those who stayed with the Church find a new religious commitment (a second naïveté, in Ricoeur's language) where a more mature understanding of the frailty and sinfulness of the Church develops, as well as an appreciation of the Church's potential for grace and life.

According to Ricoeur, as they make sense of life, people have to move beyond the stage of critique to develop a post-critical understanding of its truth. There is much in this analysis that is helpful for those responsible for the curriculum of the Catholic school. The curriculum should teach students the skills of critical thinking, but Catholic education is more than this. Students should be critical in their approach, but they must also be educated to look for truth and meaning in the subjects they study. Ricoeur's analysis of post-critical belief illuminates this challenge.

activity

Identify an area of curriculum where Ricoeur's three phases of meaning-making are evident: initial naïve understanding, critical engagement, post-critical understanding.

Post-critical belief

As part of the Leuven research project, Dirk Hutsebaut developed the Post-Critical Belief Scale that is used by many Catholic schools to profile the religious identity options taken by members of the school community (Pollefeyt & Bouwens, 2010). The scale is based on two dimensions: Symbolic vs Literal and Belief vs Disbelief.

The four quadrants in the Post-Critical Belief Scale are discussed in turn, starting at the bottom right and moving around in a clockwise direction. A Literal Believer is inclined towards fundamentalism because while there is an openness to religious faith, there is an attitude that God can be known directly and absolutely through particular literal interpretations of Scriptures and dogmas. In the next quadrant (External Critique), religious truths are still interpreted literally but they are rejected. For example, texts in the Bible are interpreted literally and Christian faith is rejected because it is seen to be ridiculous. The next quadrant (Relativity) refers to a non-believer who understands the world symbolically. People in this quadrant reject religious truth claims and hold the view that everyone's understanding is merely an interpretation because there is no God or transcendent reality really there beyond the particular opinions or beliefs of the individual. Religion is tolerated by those who take this option but religious claims to truth are seen as being misguided.

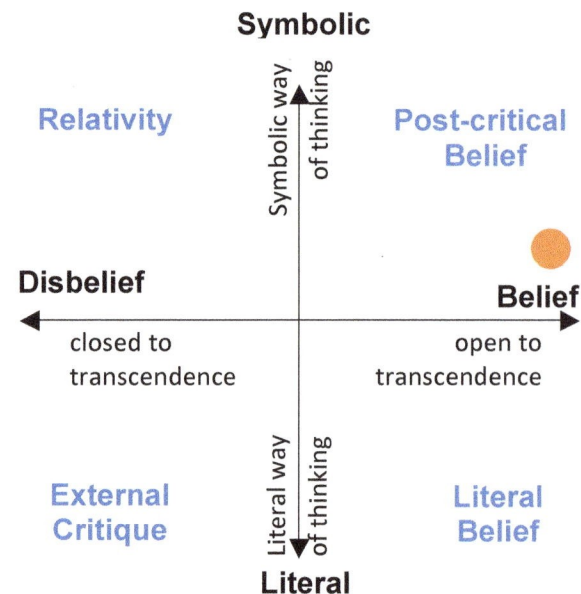

FIGURE 1: Post-Critical Belief Scale – developed from Pollefeyt and Bouwens (2010)

The fourth and preferred option in the scale is Post-critical Belief. An orange circle has been placed in this quadrant to represent the preferred position by the Leuven researchers. As can be seen, the preferred position is relatively low on symbolic interpretation but high on faith in a transcendent God. The Leuven researchers argue for a low symbolic position because they want to emphasise the point that while truth is always interpreted, it is knowable nonetheless. Over-emphasising interpretation and criticism can lead to relativism or nihilism.

The implication of post-critical belief for those who design and deliver curriculum in a Catholic school is that truth and meaning is disclosed in each of the learning areas, even though that truth is always known through criticism and interpretation. Our knowledge of the truth is always mediated through experience, stories, rituals, theories, research, traditions, institutions, churches, ministries, communities and social organisations. Post-critical believers are open to truth claims but understand that the claims must always be interpreted, rather than directly grasped.

It is not possible to explore any further here how these elements of interpretation, critique, truth and meaning flow through the curriculum of the Catholic school. Suffice to say that those who develop curriculum are equipped for their roles when they understand the necessity of critical engagement and interpretation but also have a vision of curriculum that draws from Catholic faith to find truth, meaning and hope in the midst of every learning area.

reflection

▲ How well do teachers in your school understand the relationship between interpretation and truth?

▲ Do they know how to lead students effectively into critical engagement and then beyond it into a post-critical appreciation of truth?

Designing the Catholic curriculum

I encountered a good example of a Catholic approach to curriculum recently in a Year 2 science unit on the origins of the Universe. After the class had been studying the Big Bang theory, the teacher called for volunteers to meet in a smaller group to discuss the question: Which came first, God or the Big Bang? Their discussion was videoed and became a stimulus for further conversation with the whole class. The students addressed some deep philosophical questions in quite sophisticated ways during this exercise, and the teacher noted that our young people are often more capable than we give them credit for. She also expressed the view that she felt learning generally, and learning in the religious domain in particular, was more engaging for the students when they had an issue that meant something to them and where there were various points of views that could be debated with some energy and challenge.

I know of other teachers who claim that some of their best teaching in the religious domain happens in their English classes, where the great themes of life are explored at depth by students as they study novels and analyse what they see unfolding in the characters they are studying. The Religious Education classroom provides obvious opportunities for the students to engage with the Catholic tradition of faith, but the whole curriculum in the Catholic school – which includes what happens inside the classroom and what happens beyond it – can become a means by which the school leads the students to discover what the Gospel might mean for them today.

The art of good curriculum design is to take students on a journey that does not become repetitive or boring because the students feel that they are travelling around the same tired loop. Good curriculum needs to be coherent rather than ad hoc and progressive rather than repetitious so that learning in one year builds on the foundations of prior years and leads naturally into what will follow. The curriculum needs to take students somewhere worthwhile over the thirteen years of their schooling. Teachers must be clear on the purpose of the curriculum and set strong expectations for their students. They do this by inviting students into learning experiences that are developmentally-appropriate and tailored for their learning needs. For this to happen, all available expertise needs to be applied to the curriculum developed by state authorities so that every school, including every Catholic school, has the best space possible in which to develop curriculum at the local level.

The Catholic school curriculum needs to be based not only on the state curriculum but also on the basis of a significant engagement with the living values and beliefs of a Catholic worldview. This means as a minimum that students emerge from a Catholic school with a worldview that is informed by Catholic beliefs and values in relation to God, life-giving relationships, justice and an ongoing search for what is good, right and true in their culture and world. Such objectives apply to all curriculum areas and embrace the whole staff of a Catholic school. The role played by diocesan or congregational authorities in regard to the religious dimension of curriculum also needs to be understood and respected by those who lead curriculum in the Catholic school.

The requirements for good curriculum demand a range of sophisticated skills and knowledge, and a school has no right to enrol students if it lacks the technical abilities needed to create and deliver a well-structured and engaging curriculum. Similarly, there is no point having a Catholic school if the religious dimension of school life is not at least as professionally designed and delivered as the 'secular' subjects. A range of technical skills is required by those who would rise to this challenge, but even more important than the techniques and knowledge are the faith, hope and love that a person needs if he or she is to contribute effectively to the mission of the Catholic school in our day. The chapter on staff formation which follows opens up some reflections on this issue.

A Catholic place

- ▲ Do you agree that Catholic educators should develop curriculum from a 'Catholic place'?

- ▲ A list of values like the following was proposed in a workshop where we were considering what the Catholic place might look like: protecting human life, protecting freedom and protecting dignity.

- ▲ What are some of the features of the 'Catholic place' from your perspective?

- ▲ Catholic faith cannot be reduced to a list of values like those above. What features other than values might be prominent in your understanding of the Catholic place?

- ▲ How do these features shape the curriculum in your school?

- ▲ Is there any chance that students in your school could become bored with the Catholic place in your school because they are being taken around the same 'Jesus loop' in different ways over their years in the Religious Education classroom?

Pedagogy

We focus in this chapter on Catholic pedagogy as distinct from pedagogy more widely. It is important from the outset, however, to acknowledge that good pedagogy is good pedagogy, whether it be enacted in a Catholic school or in any other type of school. Catholic pedagogy is only different because it is harnessed in the service of the mission of the Catholic school and because it is animated by Catholic understandings of culture, the human person and creation more broadly. If the research into pedagogy indicates that our twenty-first century students learn best when they have agency as learners, when they are treated as learning partners and when learning is 'real-world', then these characteristics should shape the pedagogies enacted in a Catholic school, just as they should in other types of schools.

What is distinctive about Catholic pedagogy? This question could be answered in many different ways and it is only possible to explore Catholic pedagogy from a limited number of vantage points in this chapter. We begin by considering a model developed in Belgium that considers pedagogy under the three headings of Witness, Specialist and Moderator. We then consider pedagogy beyond the classroom and the evocative expression 'divine pedagogy' and its implications for Catholic education. The distinction between Catholic pedagogy and indoctrination is considered briefly before the chapter concludes with a consideration of a religious identity profiling instrument called the *Victoria Scale*.

What is Catholic pedagogy?

- ▲ Recall any encounters you have had with effective and meaningful pedagogy. What effect did these have on the learning process for you or the students?

- ▲ There are many definitions of pedagogy. Find some definitions that are used in your school and discuss the merits of the definitions with other members of your school community.

- ▲ Discuss with some other members of your school community how the mission of your school influences the pedagogies that are used in it. Examine your school's Mission Statement to see what the implications are for pedagogy.

- ▲ Brainstorm what you think the Catholic understandings are of culture, the human person and creation more generally. How might these understandings shape the pedagogies used in your school?

- ▲ Is Catholic pedagogy reflected in your schools' pedagogical framework? If not, how can Catholic pedagogy be more explicitly visible in the framework?

- ▲ Work with some other members of your school community to develop a short statement that defines Catholic pedagogy from your perspective.

- ▲ If you have access to technology and an application like Padlet you could post your group's statement on the Wall and review all the other statements of Catholic pedagogy posted there. A collective statement of Catholic pedagogy that meets the agreement of your school community could be drafted. This process might be undertaken on a small scale at a staff meeting or it could be a far-reaching process that includes students and the wider school community.

Belgium WSM pedagogy

The Belgian analysis is that Catholic pedagogy requires the teacher to be a Witness, a Specialist and a Moderator – hence the WSM label (Pollefeyt, 2008). As *witnesses*, teachers stand ready to lead religious conversations, sharing of themselves and their experiences as appropriate for the learning process. In order to be able to do this, teachers must have an experience of faith and be in touch with the 'treasure within'. As *moderators*, teachers act as guides, leaving their students free to make their own choices. They avoid presenting their experiences as the singular path to truth. Moderators know how to create spaces that provide deep encounters with both the cultural and faith traditions and encourage the students to wrestle with their own issues in their search for meaning. An important facet of the moderator role lies in encouraging students to identify the inconsistencies and contradictions between their own views and alternative positions as the contradictions become evident in the material being studied or in the discussion of it in class.

Teachers do not simply direct the traffic of classroom learning, they should be sufficiently immersed in the cultural and faith traditions to explicitly teach their students. Teachers should also know the terrain of the learning area well enough to offer options

FIGURE 2: WSM model developed from Pollefeyt, 2008

to students or quickly recognise incomplete or inconsistent understandings when they become evident in their learning.

Teachers are only free to witness to the faith tradition and moderate the engagement of students with it if they have a deep understanding of the tradition themselves. In this sense teachers are *specialists* as they accompany students in the construction of their religious identity. Some background in theology and Scripture as well as ongoing processes of professional learning are important steps along the way for teachers in arriving at post-critical belief.

> **activity**
>
> One of the responses I have heard leaders make to the WSM model is that it could be threatening for staff who do not come from a Catholic background. Reflect on the profile of teachers on your staff and consider how comfortable they would be operating as Witnesses, Moderators and Specialists. What formation would be helpful to them in fulfilling these roles?

Sometimes a student/teacher interaction can contain within it elements of each role in WSM pedagogy. For example, I was talking with a teacher recently about a student who had said that he had stopped believing in God. The teacher acted as a Moderator by creating a space where the student felt free to disclose the reason why he had stopped believing in God – because he did not believe that the world was created in seven days. The teacher responded by sharing her understanding of the relationship between faith, science and the creation narrative in Genesis. When the teacher conveyed her understandings of biblical genre, creation theology and scientific theories of evolution, she was fulfilling the Specialist role. She was also a Witness when she shared some of her beliefs – but in so doing she was careful not to compromise her role as a Moderator – thus ensuring that the student was able to develop his own understanding, rather than having a viewpoint imposed upon him.

Pedagogy beyond teaching

Those who work in Catholic schools are witnesses whenever they care for the students and whenever they go the extra mile for them, especially the students who are most difficult to befriend and include in the life of the school. The witness that staff give to their faith may not always be explicit, but the mission of the school is only fully realised when students regularly encounter explicit faith witnesses from at least some of the staff they engage with at school. Every member of staff encountered by students at the school must, however, support the school's Catholic ethos. Pedagogy does not start and end in the classroom.

All staff have the opportunity to 'teach' the students – even if only by the way they interact with them and attend to their wellbeing. Catholic schools seek to form the student's worldview, which embraces how they think, what they value and how they feel. This being the case, sometimes the most important learning outcomes for students are not in the domain of new skills or knowledge.

For example, a student in one of our schools had a number of social challenges and was on the edges, not fitting in so well with his peers. He also needed things to be 'fun', and learning was not on his fun list. With this in mind, his teacher gave him a camera and a clipboard and asked him to interview some people of his own choosing about a topic of interest to him. The teacher's intention was to help the student build relationships and re-engage with his peers. She used the technology to blur the boundaries between learning and having fun. In this sense she opened up a frontier space where the student moved out of his comfort zone into a space where the wall between fun and learning could be broken down. Her knowledge of the student and her grasp of good pedagogy enabled her to re-engage the student with his learning and with his peers.

Divine pedagogy

The evocative phrase 'divine pedagogy' is used in Church documents on religious formation. The General Directory for Catechesis (GDC) employed a rich series of images to describe the divine pedagogy, indicating that faith formation processes should follow the example of God, whose self-disclosure unfolded progressively over time. God uses language that humans can understand, and we should do likewise, using accessible language to communicate the Gospel to members of our local community. God's word is mysterious and revealed progressively in a number of ways, not all at once, to the believer. The WSM approach outlined above provides one way of modelling this 'divine pedagogy', and teachers and schools are faithful to their mission when they take up this model or one that is complementary to it.

It is also important that those who design and enact the religious dimension of curriculum in a Catholic school understand that ultimately *religious formation is God's work*, and it unfolds at its most basic level as an experience of grace in the life of each person in the school community. Religious outcomes cannot be scheduled or programmed, they can only be encouraged and supported. A key responsibility for those who lead Catholic schools is to ensure that religious beliefs and practices are continuously and appropriately interpreted so that they are intelligible to their community. School and system leaders should also understand that God's revelation occurs mysteriously and progressively in the lives of people, and that religious outcomes cannot be imposed from the outside, they can only be stimulated and scaffolded with the students, and they are necessarily the product of dialogue. Religious formation is as much an encounter with grace as it is an experience of a series of activities structured by those who are committed to proclaiming the Gospel in the context of a school.

A Catholic pedagogy that does not indoctrinate

One of the key challenges that educators in a Catholic school face is to enact a pedagogy that invites students into a strong encounter with what it means to be Catholic without trampling inappropriately upon their religious diversity or allowing the educational process to degenerate into indoctrination.

The frontier space between religious formation, relativism, secularism and indoctrination is tricky to navigate, but with the right support, Catholic educators whom I have worked with can find their way through the landscape without too much difficulty. In many cases, having navigated a way through themselves, they are able to help both students and their parents do the same.

Catholic pedagogy as dialogue – the Victoria Scale

I have found the pedagogical options presented in a religious identity profiling instrument called the *Victoria Scale* very helpful in providing Catholic educators with some important compass bearings when it comes to planning faith formation processes.

The Scale was developed as part of the Leuven/CECV project by Pollefeyt and Bouwens and is based on a typology created by ter Horst and Hermans (Pollefeyt & Bouwens, 2010). The scale comprises two dimensions: solidarity and Catholic identity. 'Solidarity' refers to the extent to which the Catholic school is open to meaning systems other than the Catholic worldview. 'Catholic

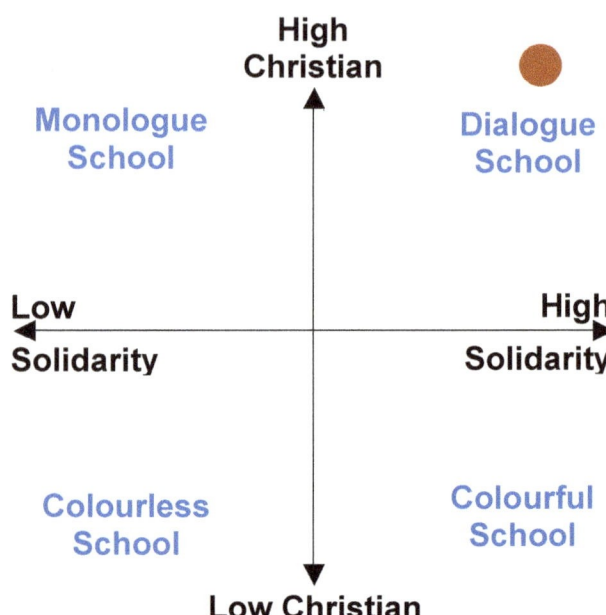

FIGURE 3: Pollefeyt & Bouwens (2010)

identity' measures the extent to which members of the school community live out of a generally shared Catholic inspiration. Schools with high solidarity allow a strong engagement to occur with non-Catholic beliefs, whereas schools with low solidarity discourage this engagement. A school with a high Catholic identity and a low solidarity is called a 'Monologue School' in the Victoria Scale because the Catholic voice is the only one that is allowed to sound in the public spaces of the school. Other voices are suppressed. Schools that avoid any public commitment to religion are low in both solidarity and Catholic identity and are called 'Colourless Schools' in the Scale. Religion is seen as a private matter in secular cultures and therefore is not a suitable topic for discussion in a public forum such as a school. Despite their religious raison d'être, Catholic schools can be susceptible to becoming colourless schools if the leaders are not vigilant, because the forces of secularism can push teachers away from spaces where religious commitment is discussed with students.

'Colourful Schools' are places where diversity is recognised and celebrated and where discussions involving faith and meaning are encouraged but no particular religious viewpoint is privileged. Colourful Schools are high on solidarity but low on Catholic identity in the Victoria Scale. Everyone is encouraged to share their views, and there is no commitment on the part of the school to advance any particular religious agenda. In this type of school, Catholic beliefs sit equally alongside the religious and non-religious meaning systems espoused by members of the school community. While this type of school celebrates diversity and pluralism, it does not provide a sustained and systematic encounter with Catholic beliefs or practices.

The 'Dialogue School' is the fourth and final option presented in the Victoria Scale, and it is the one that is seen as being appropriate for pedagogies employed in the Catholic school. The Dialogue School is high in both Catholic identity and Solidarity. While the viewpoints of all students are respected, there is a clear commitment to providing a systematic and sustained engagement with Catholic beliefs or teachings. Those who take the dialogue option know how to engage students with Catholic beliefs and values without imposing these beliefs and values on the students. They also know how to create spaces where the students feel free to share their own understandings and viewpoints, even as they engage with the Catholic story.

Conclusion

The topic of pedagogy in any school is very rich, broad and deep. Catholic pedagogy draws from the best of contemporary pedagogical theory and considers the issues from a Catholic perspective. Those who lead Catholic schools fulfil an important element of their role when they ensure that the professional learning programs for staff continually improve their understandings of the mission of the school and its implications for the pedagogies enacted in partnership with students. With this in mind it is appropriate that staff formation is considered in the next chapter.

reflection

▲ What is distinctive about Catholic pedagogy?

▲ How well does your school prepare teachers for their roles as witnesses, moderators or specialists?

▲ Are these roles the most important roles associated with Catholic pedagogy?

▲ What are the opportunities and constraints that twenty-first century pedagogies present for realising the mission of the Catholic school?

This chapter on Staff Formation begins in a strange place by referring to a superannuation television advertisement. The advertisement opens with a pair of office workers travelling upwards on two escalators. The worker on the superannuation product being advertised travels faster and further on their escalator than the other person who represents the alternative product. That image stays with me as I reflect on the journeys that different staff members take when they are employed in our schools. Some schools take staff into very rich formative spaces, whereas staff in other schools experience programs that are barren by comparison.

Over the course of the chapters of this book thus far we have named many qualities and capabilities that are needed if a school is to have a strong and vibrant Catholic identity. Educators have been presented as storytellers who draw richly from elements of religion such as sacred texts and rituals to lead their students into an appreciation of Catholic faith. This faith is only experienced as authentic by students when staff offer good pastoral care and demonstrate a commitment to justice. In the chapter on Jesus we explored the challenge that teachers face in opening up spaces where students are confronted with Jesus' question: Who do you say that I am? One of the challenges here is for the curriculum to be structured well enough so that the question does not become predictable and alienating for students. The task is also to avoid reducing Jesus to being merely a 'good man' who preached values such as friendship or forgiveness. Students are entitled to be led into the meaning of Christian mysteries such as

Orientation

Recall your time as a teacher in Catholic education. On a personal timeline, plot what have been significant informal or formal staff formation experiences for you in the Catholic identity area. Share with a partner and identify why the plotted experiences stand out. Bring this reflective journey to the reading of the chapter.

the resurrection, the Trinity, grace and the sacraments during their time in a Catholic school. Teachers need to be knowledgeable, skilled and committed if these challenges are to be met.

The importance of encounter, rather than imposition, and creativity, rather than replication, was highlighted in the Frontier chapter. School leaders require courage, knowledge, faith and wisdom as they move into frontier spaces with their communities. These frontier spaces are opened up when members of the school community move out of the settled territory of the traditional ways of expressing Catholic identity and into unexplored territory with staff and students whose worlds can seem somewhat alien to Catholic faith as we have known it. We saw in the Liturgy and Prayer chapter that each Catholic school needs staff who know the liturgical tradition well enough to make it richly available to their colleagues. The reflections on divine pedagogy and the WSM model in the Pedagogy chapter explored how to be in the frontier with students by exercising the roles of Witness, Specialist and Moderator. The Curriculum chapter presented teaching as a dance between culture, truth, interpretation, relativism, nihilism and post-critical belief.

The capabilities required for working in the spaces that have just been described need to be developed within the context of rich programs of staff formation. We are only halfway through the book and I can assure you that there are many more facets yet of Catholic identity which need to be explored, so there are more capabilities to come! How can staff formation programs equip staff for the critical roles they play in our schools?

Strategic staff formation

Programs of staff formation cannot focus on everything all at the same time. A strategic approach to staff formation focuses on the most important areas first and leaves the other areas to later. Formation programs are most effective when resources are targeted to the areas that are most in need. The importance of mapping current capabilities and identifying priority areas for strengthening and improvement is underscored here. Those who design and deliver effective staff formation experiences know their school communities intimately, they understand the strengths and weaknesses of their staff, and they ensure that the required capabilities and dispositions are built up over time in processes which take staff somewhere worthwhile over the journey by being creative, engaging and authentically Catholic.

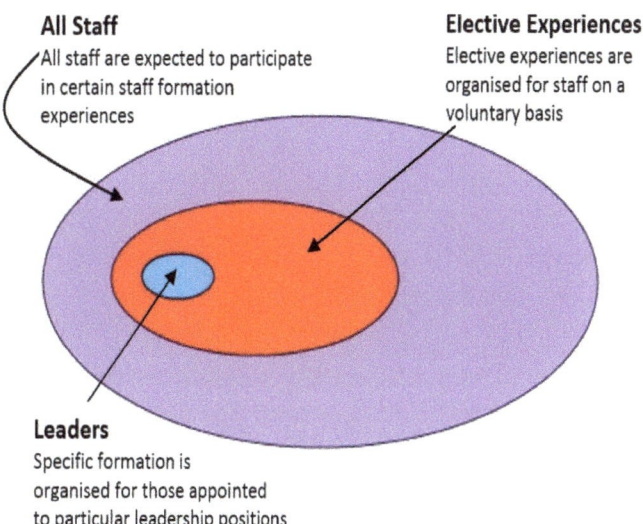

All Staff
All staff are expected to participate in certain staff formation experiences

Elective Experiences
Elective experiences are organised for staff on a voluntary basis

Leaders
Specific formation is organised for those appointed to particular leadership positions

Effective staff formation programs rest on the firm understanding that staff come from a wide variety of backgrounds. Some staff members have been Catholic from birth, whereas others have almost no familiarity or affinity with Catholic beliefs, rituals or values. All staff, however, by virtue of their employment, embrace a commitment to support the school's ethos and religious identity. A critical task for each school then is to offer a formation experience for staff that equips them for their roles, even in the diversity of their backgrounds and experiences.

Each school system and each school leader must be clear about their expectations of staff in terms of their ongoing formation for mission. The diagram above highlights the importance of clarity regarding the requirements for all staff, as well as the formation that is organised for people in particular roles and the elective experiences that might be taken up voluntarily by staff. Some of these requirements and experiences might be developed at the system level, whereas others might be instituted at the school level.

To be effective across a career in Catholic education it is important that teachers accept some *personal responsibility* for their own religious formation. At the same time there is a *school responsibility* to ensure all staff are equipped to contribute effectively to the mission of the local school. The local bishop or religious order authority also has a responsibility to ensure that the diocesan mission or religious order's charism is nurtured and strengthened by the staff who are employed in the school. The way in which these three levels of responsibility are fulfilled has an important bearing on how Catholic identity is built and sustained over time.

activity

Map the formative experiences that all staff access at your school, as well as the experiences that are offered as electives to staff according to their particular interests or needs. Include the formation in your map that people in particular roles in your school need to undertake as a requirement for their roles.

▲ Are there particularly strong experiences that appear on your map?

▲ Are there experiences that are missing or could be strengthened?

▲ Are there experiences that have outlived their usefulness and could be replaced by something more contemporary?

▲ What new ideas could be adopted?

In the light of this analysis, what changes would you like to make to the staff formation program at your school?

A formation of the heart

Leaders should remember that while knowledge is important, commitment and love are even more critical. St Bonaventure argued in the thirteenth century that people should ask for grace, not instruction; fire, not light. Without downplaying the need for knowledge or technique, those who are responsible for designing programs of formation for staff must focus first on the heart, not on the mind, as personal experience is often a necessary condition for nurturing knowledge. If staff develop an appreciation of the implications of Catholic faith for school life, they will be led to deepen their understanding of it. Knowledge without love does not enable someone to contribute authentically to the religious identity of the Catholic school.

The development of a spirituality that can sustain the religious commitment of staff is essential if staff members are to grow in their capacity to bear witness to the Gospel. As noted in the Catholic Identity chapter, philosopher Paul Ricoeur's analysis is that identity is acquired via the detour of narratives, symbols and metaphors. When members of the school community share experiences of God and grace with each other, the outcomes can be quite deep and powerful. They no longer see themselves as observers of the unfolding Catholic story but as active participants in its evolution.

The strategies used to engage staff are many and varied. A school leader spoke to me about a staff member who had become very alienated from anything religious in the school and was known for his negativity towards activities such as liturgies or retreat days. The leader said that he made the effort to go to the airport to farewell a group being led by the alienated staff member. After the trip the staff member expressed his appreciation of the leader's effort to come and farewell his students. Over time, the leader noticed that the staff member's alienation from the religious life of the school had begun to dissipate. The staff member's attitude and engagement began to shift slowly and subtly from that point forward. He began to participate positively in religious activities in a way that was remarked upon by others. The school leader believed that because someone had shown an interest in the alienated staff member as a person, and because the contribution he was making to the life of the school was affirmed, the alienated member of staff was able to associate that care and interest with the religious identity of the school. It began to mean something positive to him.

Pope Francis speaks about 'taking the first step and becoming involved'. The following passage says something important to those who organise staff formation processes in schools:

> Let us try a little harder to take the first step and become involved. An evangelising community gets involved by word and deed in people's daily lives; it bridges distances ... and it embraces human life, touching the suffering flesh of Christ in others. Evangelisers thus take on the 'smell of the sheep' and the sheep are willing to hear their voice. An evangelizing community is also supportive, standing by people at every step of the way, no matter how difficult or lengthy this may prove to be (Evangelii Gaudium, # 24).

Although retreat days and formal programs of staff formation are important, the preparedness of school leaders to become involved in the lives of their staff can be even more significant, and this is true in turn of staff in relation to the students and families in the school. Engaging with people authentically and reaching out to them can sometimes produce very positive and unexpected results. The engagement does not always need to occur at dramatic times such as the death of a family member; it can occur in low-key and unheralded ways daily in the life of the school.

One of the simplest engagement strategies that I have experienced is to invite a member of staff to be interviewed in a staff meeting about their perceptions of the Catholic identity of the school and what it means to them. Deliberately choosing staff who have quite different stories and relationships to the Catholic Church can give rise to very rich sessions when there is an appropriate environment of trust and goodwill. Over numbers of such interviews, the richness of the ways in which staff see Catholic identity and contribute to it can become evident in new and refreshing ways.

activity

Create a forum where voices of the school community can be heard as they discuss their perceptions of the Catholic identity of the school and what it means to them. One approach would be for members of the community to be interviewed at a staff meeting. The voices could include staff, parents and students. Another approach would be to compile a video and show it at a meeting of staff or the school board or to students in class. Choose community members with quite different stories and relationships to the Catholic Church.

The WSM model and staff

The WSM model mentioned in the Pedagogy chapter does not just apply to students; it is relevant to staff formation. Religious beliefs cannot be imposed on staff, any more than on students. Faith is a gift from God that must be received in freedom. It takes skill and sensitivity to structure experiences that invite staff into encounters that are rich in possibility for religious commitment to be developed. Formative and freeing spaces are constructed by those who know how to act as Witnesses and Moderators. Witnesses share their faith authentically, appropriately and naturally. Moderators do not seek to compel or manipulate staff to adopt religious teachings; they seek to create the conditions where cogent invitations into a Catholic vision of life and creation are offered to staff regularly in the life of the school. These invitations, offered over years of employment in a Catholic school, enable staff to contribute more effectively to the school's mission. This contribution will vary considerably among staff according to their roles and life experiences.

The third element of the WSM model was that of the Specialist, who has the knowledge required if staff formation programs are to be authentically Catholic at the same time as they are culturally resonant. Schools and systems have a particular responsibility for building Catholic identity by helping staff grow in their understanding of the culture within which they live and the opportunities and constraints it presents for witnessing to religious faith. Those who lead formation programs in schools work in a context that is characterised by pluralism when it comes to the cultural traditions and backgrounds of staff. It is within this pluralist context that each member of staff fashions out their unique and authentic contribution to the Catholic ethos of the school.

You can learn a great deal about a Catholic school by asking questions about its staff formation program. I visited a school recently where the principal and Religious Education coordinator spoke enthusiastically about an initiative they had taken with staff prayer. Data from some research they had been doing with staff had confronted the Leadership Team with the reality that while their staff engaged in verbal prayer, there was little knowledge or appreciation of inner forms of prayer such as meditation. There was a lack of dedicated sacred space in the school and a sense that prayer was not as deep as it could be. Each staff member was issued with a prayer journal and asked to bring it along to a 15 minute staff prayer session that was instituted as part of the staff meeting. Staff members each took turns to lead a session and were encouraged to explore new ways of praying traditional prayers in the context of the Gospel of the day.

I found myself wondering, as this initiative was described, whether there were any staff members who would have issues with this requirement for one reason or another. It seemed apparent, however, that the initiative had been well-received, and this had a lot to do with the relational style of the leaders at the school.

reflection

▲ What kind of a journey does the staff formation program in your school take staff on?

▲ Do you target your resources to develop the capabilities that are most critical at this time?

▲ Do you offer the right mix of mandatory experiences for all staff alongside optional experiences for staff with particular needs or interests?

Ecological Conversion

The images below were taken at a school that has a deep appreciation of the powerful role that the environment can play in enhancing learning outcomes for students. Each year the younger students are given marigold seeds, and they watch the seeds germinate and grow into flowers as the first term unfolds. The marigold exercise is timed to coincide with Lent and Easter. In the lead up to Ash Wednesday the students are invited to notice the garden beds, which once contained beautiful flowers and now appear to be dry and dead. After an Ash Wednesday liturgy the students plant seeds in the barren tubs. During Lent they learn about the resurrection of Jesus, the promise of new life with God, and how despair turned to hope and courage for the followers of Jesus.

The Leadership Team at the school is very clear that marigolds are not the focus in the garden learning experience. Jesus is the focus. The students are invited to reflect on the delight and hope of new life as they hear the story of Jesus' resurrection. One of the school leaders offered the following reflection on the purpose of the unit from his perspective:

This is a story that asks us to trust in the promise of new life – the new beginnings that occur in small and large ways every day, even in the most difficult of times. At our school, the students are constantly noticing this cycle of life, death, change, and new life whether in the garden, in the life cycle of butterflies or in the ways they see themselves and their relationships change.

I was rather taken with the question which emerged during a discussion I had with the school's Leadership Team: 'How can we be sure that this unit is about Jesus, not marigolds?' I believe this question needs to be asked any time a strategy is employed where some aspect of human experience provides a background and basis for understanding some aspect of Christian faith.

The beauty of creation can lead to an appreciation of the Reign of God

Pope John Paul II often referred to ecological themes in his addresses and encouraged an 'ecological conversion', leading to a fuller sense of the closeness of the relationship between human beings and the natural environment. In the prayer after the First Reading of the Easter Vigil, the 'wonderful beauty and order' of creation is affirmed and a connection is made with the Kingdom or Reign of God that Jesus proclaimed. This Kingdom was described as being equal and even superior to the creation of the world. The Kingdom of God is a new and definitive intervention that consists not only of liberation from oppression but also the gladness and joy that comes from surrendering oneself to God.

Curriculum units or learning activities which begin with human experience but fail to connect explicitly with Christian beliefs associated with that experience run the risk of hollowing out Christian faith and secularising it. This is the case whether the unit is exploring a creation theme or themes in reconciliation, justice or what it means to experience a loving human relationship.

Teachers who appreciate the richness of the tradition are able to work with human themes in Catholic ways by engaging the students explicitly with teachings, narratives or practices related to them. The marigold unit is not just about beauty and looking after the environment, important as these themes are. The unit considers the environment from the vantage point of Christian faith. Creation is a reflection of God's beauty, and it is seen as being valuable not just because of its importance for our quality of life but because it is a sacred reflection of the God from whom all creation comes.

The ASSISI Framework

The Assisi Framework can be found in a document called *On Holy Ground* available at the Catholic Earthcare website. In each category of the Framework, identify elements within your school that show a commitment to ecological conversion in the school community. Work with some interested members of the school community to explore opportunities for growth and change to strengthen and maintain this commitment.

Ecological conversion is more than hugging trees

I once shared a meal with a bishop and a number of teachers from the school I was working in at the time. It was a very stimulating meal where we discussed a number of Church issues, and at one point the conversation became quite heated as we discussed the relationship between Catholic beliefs and environmental sustainability. The bishop was highly critical of what he saw happening in schools where the students and teachers were into 'hugging trees', as he saw it. He felt the emphasis on the environment was a popularist betrayal of the religious formation that should have been offered to students in a Catholic school.

Of course it is possible to teach environmental themes 'horizontally' without mentioning God or Christian faith. It is also possible to draw deeply from the wells of the tradition to explore what ecological conversion might mean when seen through the eyes of religious commitment. A consultant was telling me recently about his work with teachers to support their learning in this area. He invited teachers to engage with the Genesis creation narratives and the work of Walter Brueggemann (2010). These narratives have traditionally been interpreted as supporting a view of the human person standing over and above creation, using and abusing it for their own purposes. Brueggemann makes the case that the Genesis narratives encourage a view of the human person as a vital participant in creation but only in the context of being in harmony with it. The paradigm shifts from domination to right relationships.

Sacred places and relationships

▲ Create a collage of images, stories or artefacts about a place you experience as sacred. Share with the wider group.

▲ Create a collage of images, stories or artefacts about a relationship you experience as sacred. Share with wider group.

▲ What is it that makes these places/relationships sacred?

The consultant went on to say that he uses the Prologue from John's Gospel to invite teachers to consider how creation reflects the divinity of Jesus. 'All things came into being through him, and without him not one thing came into being' (John 1:3). The General Directory for Catechesis observes that there is often too much emphasis given to the humanity of Jesus without enough attention being paid to his divinity (GDC, # 30). Through the theme of creation, teachers are given a unique opportunity to encounter a high Christology and its significance for Christian life. I wish that I had heard this story before the dinner party with the 'tree-hugging' bishop as I would have been very interested to hear what his views might have been on such a strategy.

Personal and communal implications

Ask yourself what the implications of the texts below are for you personally. The Scripture texts can be found in the Bible and the texts from the popes are available at the Vatican website.

▲ Genesis 1

▲ John 1:3

▲ Joint Statement of John Paul II and The Ecumenical Patriarch His Holiness Bartholomew I
  › What is required is an act of repentance on our part and a renewed attempt to view ourselves, one another, and the world around us within the perspective of the divine design for creation. The problem is not simply economic and technological; it is moral and spiritual. A solution at the economic and technological level can be found only if we undergo, in the most radical way, an inner change of heart, which can lead to a change in lifestyle and of unsustainable patterns of consumption and production. A genuine conversion in Christ will enable us to change the way we think and act.

▲ Homily from the Mass of Inauguration of Pope Francis 19 March 2013
  › The vocation of being a 'protector', however, is not just something involving us Christians alone; it also has a prior dimension which is simply human, involving everyone. It means protecting all creation, the beauty of the created world, as the Book of Genesis tells us and as Saint Francis of Assisi showed us. It means respecting each of God's creatures and respecting the environment in which we live. It means protecting people, showing loving concern for each and every person, especially children, the elderly, those in need, who are often the last we think about.

Work with a colleague to explore the implications of these texts for your school community.

Family, Parish and School

Partnerships between school and family

Parents are affirmed in Church documents as the 'primary and principal educators' of their children, and a feature of the way a Catholic school operates therefore must be the strength of the support given to the educative role of the parents. In recent years all schools, not just Catholic schools, have been challenged to strengthen family and community engagement in student learning and the life of the school. The seven dimensions in the Family Schools Partnerships Framework provide a good starting place for anyone wanting to think through the relationship between the school and the family. The following dimensions of the framework map out the territory that any school leader might consider when reflecting on the quality of the family school partnership: communication, connecting learning at home and school, building community and identity, recognising the role of the family, consultative decision-making, collaborating beyond school and participation.

The issues that arise across these dimensions are many and varied and fall well beyond the scope of this chapter. The focus here is with a very specific issue: the relationship between family, school and parish. Changes in family and parish life have profoundly affected the relationships between the Catholic school and its parish and family relationships, so much so that it is time for some significant re-imagining to occur.

Rethinking the relationships between home, parish and school

I once heard a Canon lawyer say, 'You can't be Catholic on your own' and this point strikes me as being very important when it comes to reflecting on the Catholic school's religious identity. With whom is the school being Catholic, other than itself?

Pope Francis has highlighted in Evangelii Gaudium the 'great flexibility' of the parish, saying 'it can assume quite different contours depending on the openness and missionary creativity of the pastor and the community' (Francis, 2013, # 28). The parish will be the Church living in the midst of her people when it 'really is in contact with the homes and the lives of its people, and does not become a useless structure out of touch with people or a self-absorbed group made up of a chosen few'. These are demanding words, and they challenge parishes, schools and families to reflect on their relationships and structures to be sure that they are what is most needed at this time. The Pope has invited everyone to be bold and creative in this task of renewal and rethinking. I offer the following reflections in that spirit.

Three forms of partnership between parish and school

When I visit a Catholic school, one of the things I look out for is how the school relates to the broader Church. Three patterns of relationships have emerged for me as I have reflected on what I have seen.

The first form of partnership understands Church to be the community that gathers in a parish on a Sunday and does not see the Catholic school as having an ecclesial identity. The school is Catholic to the extent that its families are in Church on Sunday. The problem with this form of partnership is that the religious identity of the Catholic school rests on factors which are beyond the control of the school. Whatever else they might be good at, schools have little or no control over what families decide to do on a Sunday. For the most part, they also have little control over what the parish offers those families who do attend.

I know many school leaders who have this reality in mind when they say that 'the school is the Church' for most families in their schools. Empirically, it is hard

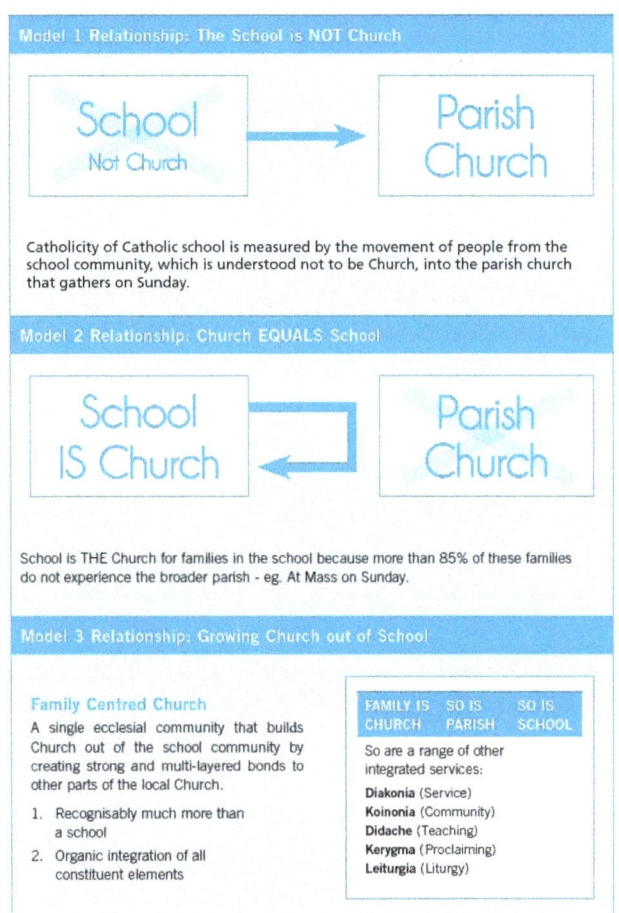

to argue with this position, which I see as the second form of partnership that has emerged over the past half-century. Most families in our schools (potenially more than 80%) are not engaged in the broader life of the Church beyond school, and if the school is seen as having an ecclesial identity it makes sense to say that school is Church for these families. There are theological and practical problems with this position though. On a theological level, it is impossible to be Catholic on one's own. One can only be Catholic when one is joined to the broader communion of the Church. On a practical level this second form of partnership fails when the student graduates from school. Essentially the student also graduates from Church in the 'school is Church' partnership model. While any number of rich formative experiences may have been offered to the students when they were at school, at the time of graduation when the enrolment ceases so do the ecclesial experiences. Students and their families no longer have a Church community that they belong to. It's all over at graduation.

The third form of partnership seeks to provide ecclesial experiences that survive graduation for school families. In this form of partnership the goal is not only to have a good relationship with the broader parish but to create community experiences which engage school families in a sustainable way with the community of the wider Church. These community experiences have many faces: they may begin in a social or a sporting arena, they may have their origins in a program of outreach or justice, they could be a cooking class, a prayer experience, a ritual or an experience of pastoral care in a time of crisis. There are two common elements in the experiences associated with this model of partnership. Firstly, they are grounded in the life of the school. The families do not have to go into a strange environment in order to access the experience; the events, relationships and programs are experienced naturally in the life of the school. Secondly, the experiences include members of the wider Church so that when a family's child graduates from school, they are still perfectly able to continue accessing the experiences if they wish to make that choice. In this model, those families who feel drawn into the Church community still have a place to go when their children graduate from the school.

The creation of these wider community experiences is deceptively difficult to orchestrate in the life of the school. Educators, strangely enough, do tend to think in schooling terms. Similarly, parish leaders often look to shift families and programs out of the school community into a 'parish' setting before they recognise the activity as being properly ecclesial. I have come to believe that the professional training of educators and parish leaders seriously circumscribes their vision and significantly inhibits their capacity to move into this third partnership model. Increasingly I believe we need to open traditional educational or pastoral approaches out into modes of practice which are informed by community development capabilities. I have developed the following 'community development wish list' for a Church team located in a school that invites school families into the broader life of the Church. Those who work in such schools demonstrate the following capabilities:

- a living faith that provides a compelling witness
- a capacity to reflect theologically from a Catholic place
- an ability to understand and appreciate the contemporary outlook and mindset of families – especially those families not currently engaged in the life of the Church beyond school

They also are able to:

- network and offer effective invitations to families, especially those families who are in special need or those who are not engaged with the life of the Church

- be creative and devise pastoral strategies and structures that connect and resonate with those families in new ways
- appreciate the Church's understanding of the unfolding stages or 'moments' of conversion – the conversion process begins with the desire of the human heart for love and beauty, then moves into discipleship, then abandonment of self in Christ and finally, moved by the Spirit and nourished by the sacraments, prayer and charity, journeying towards perfection
- build the capacity of community members so that the community develops initiatives that matter to them – as distinct from 'delivering services' to community members that professionals feel they need

I'm not suggesting that any of this is easy. As indicated, the third partnership model I have just described is deceptively difficult to orchestrate in the life of the school. It requires school and parish 'professionals' to infuse their practice with insights and principles that can initially seem feasible but ultimately are foreign to the professional training and practice of those involved. This third model will only grow out of the life of the school into the broader Church when these shifts in professional outlook have occurred. Equally challenging questions also arise in the domains of funding and governance. Colleagues I work with generally agree with my critique of the first two partnership models above but have not always been drawn to the third model I am presenting for their consideration. As you can imagine I have been quick to invite them to tell me about their Model 4. If they don't like my third model I ask them, 'What partnership model do you see as being an appropriate vessel for a ministry of outreach which invites school families into the broader life of the Church?'

Imagining new relationships

Gather together a group from the community that represents parents, parish, students and staff, and invite them to imagine how relationships might be reformulated so that the links between school, home and the wider Church are refreshed and liberated. The following process can be as large or as small as your resources allow in terms of time and the number of community members involved.

▲ Represent, in whatever way you like, your 'ideal' image of Family, Parish and School Partnership for your school community. Imagine new experiences and outreach ministry for your school's families.

▲ Consider the context, interests and expertise of your community. What motivates and excites the people in your community?

▲ Wonderings …
  › *I wonder what the students would imagine …*
  › *I wonder what the families would imagine …*
  › *I wonder what other school communities would imagine …*

What might the ideal look like?	Who might participate?	What might we need to make this happen?

As a group, select one of the possibilities that you believe could happen now. Share with other groups why the experience you've chosen is important to you.

The photo below was taken in a little village about 120 km from Dili in Timor Leste. Staff and recently graduated students from one of our schools travelled to the school to repair and paint community buildings, teach sport and dance in the local schools and assist with the health program. Why did these young adults and their teachers travel to this place, and what happened when they got there? The following comment from one of the students conveys how life-changing the experience was for those involved.

Going to bed each night knowing that we brought happiness and hope to hundreds of Timorese people that day was the most rewarding feeling in the world.

As a Catholic educator, it was inspiring to hear the recently returned group describe their immersion experience in a country where the beauty and joy of the people was palpable but the quality of life seriously impaired by a lack of material resources. It was obvious that these recently graduated students had not only lived through a profound experience, they had joined a deeply meaningful network of peers who were committed to working for justice and a better world.

In this chapter we consider experiences like these, large and small, from the perspectives of charity and justice. As the chapter advances we will consider at greater depth what is meant by 'charity' and 'justice', but at this point charity is taken to be 'the love which God

lavishes upon us and which we in turn must share with others' (Deus Caritas Est, # 1). We consider justice through the prism of the social teaching of the Church, which addresses a wide range of issues such as war and peace, poverty, human rights, the nature of the human person, family, freedom, marriage, the common good, work, politics, private property and the economy.

The link between the Reign of God that Jesus proclaimed and the commitment to work for justice and right relationships was noted in an earlier chapter. While immersion experiences such as the one described above represent particularly elaborate and intense curriculum moments, every Catholic school has the capacity to offer students opportunities to encounter others whose lives are challenging or disadvantaged for one reason or another. Some schools have disadvantage on their doorsteps, and there is no need to travel to find opportunities for the exercise of charity and justice. Other schools comprise students from relatively affluent backgrounds, and the students need to be challenged to leave their comfortable worlds behind to begin to see how life is for others.

reflection

▲ Who are the 'poor' in your school?

▲ What experience do those who are most fragile or marginal have in your school?

▲ How does your school reach out to those in need beyond the school gate?

One of the proudest moments in my own teaching occurred at a large facility for adults living with profound disabilities. I took a group of Year 11 students from my school to the facility to work in pairs and take a resident for a walk around the grounds. My challenge to the students as we arrived was to speak to their residents and engage with them, rather than simply talking to each other, thereby ignoring the residents as they pushed them around in the wheelchairs. I could see as each pair was introduced to a resident just how threatened my students were with the non-verbal person, who was physically contorted and either silent or making strange noises. A tense silence descended upon my students as they moved out into the grounds with their residents. I cannot convey how proud I was as I later observed the students from afar in the grounds, pointing out birds and other features in the landscape to the resident they were paired with.

These adolescent boys were awkward as they reached out beyond their comfort zones to engage with the residents, but it was an awkwardness that was set within a great and tender beauty. It seemed to me that they were in a frontier zone of their own making with the residents – in a place that contains 'unfamiliar and as yet unmapped, unexpected features' (Haers, 2004). I had led them to the frontier but not gone with them into it. For an educator, there are few experiences that can beat opening up such frontiers for one's students. I don't know enough about the residents to know for sure how beneficial they found their time with our students. I feel confident, however, that it was worthwhile for them because the workers at the facility assured me that getting the residents outside into the fresh air and having one-on-one attention was an all-too-infrequent luxury. I do know our students though, and I know without doubt that they had touched something deep together in a simple but profound way during the experience.

Good pedagogy demands that experiences are deepened by reflection that leads to growth and new understanding. Various categories of schools were discussed in the Pedagogy chapter and these included the Colourless School, the Colourful School, the Monologue School and the Dialogue School. The dimension of charity within the curriculum can be understood with these types of schools in mind. In a Colourless School, students may have experiences of charity but there is no attempt to draw the meaning of the experiences out into an open discourse. The ideas or feelings that students have are seen as being private to them, rather than being brought out into a public conversation. In a Monologue School, Catholic perspectives on the experiences are highlighted but other understandings or meanings are either rejected or suppressed. In a Colourful School, the students are encouraged to share their views, but Catholic perspectives are either not advanced or are subsumed by the other values or worldviews enunciated by students and the materials they are studying. In a Dialogue School, the students are encouraged to express their own views but they are very deliberately invited into a systematic engagement with Catholic beliefs and perspectives as the learning process unfolds. The Dialogue School was presented in the Pedagogy chapter as the preferred option for the Catholic school.

In a Dialogue School, students not only imagine a better world, they are challenged to consider how their aspirations might become a reality that is worthy of them and the world they want to create. A Catholic view of the human person and Catholic understandings of the meaning and purpose of the world are brought to the fore as students make meaning in their learning. One way students might process experiences in a Dialogue School is to reflect on the meaning of the following words from the Lord's Prayer in the light of what they have seen and felt during their experiences:

Our Father who art in heaven, hallowed by thy name. Thy kingdom come, thy will be done on earth as it is in heaven ...

activity

Identify moments, large and small, in the curriculum of your school where students are led out into frontier experiences with people whose lives are difficult, limited or challenging in some way. Consider how your school supports students as they grapple with the meaning of these difficulties, limitations or challenges. Consider how you help students to find their place in the challenges and what the links might be to the Gospel that Jesus proclaimed.

Not every student in a Catholic school can travel to a place like Timor Leste, but it is essential that each student is challenged to reach out beyond self-interest to give of themselves to others. Why is this so?

Charity

Christian faith cannot be reduced to an ethical choice or an idea; it is an experience of love and an encounter with the God who has become one of us in Jesus (Deus Caritas Est, # 1). The encounter and ongoing relationship with Jesus gives Christians a new horizon and a decisive direction. As was discussed in the Jesus chapter, a touchstone for the Catholic identity of the school is the witness the school gives to the place of God and Jesus in a Catholic understanding of our world and the people who live in it. A Catholic understanding of charity is that it is animated by the prior experience of God's love and a commitment to sharing this love with others. Charity is not something optional and nice for Catholics to do; it is an essential element of their religious identity. Benedict quotes St Augustine, who held that 'if you see charity, you see the Trinity'. Pope Benedict went so far to say that charity expresses the Church's deepest nature. Benedict also said that the Church can never become just another provider of social assistance: 'Practical activity will always be insufficient, unless it visibly expresses a love for [humanity], a love nourished by an encounter with Christ' (Benedict XVI, 2012, # 1).

reflection

▲ Is it enough for students to show charity to those in need, or do they need to also understand that their charity reflects God's love? In other words, should Catholic educators be satisfied that their students are loving, caring people or should we be leading students to make links between human love and God who created us in love?

In a 'Dialogue' Catholic school, the students will be encouraged to appreciate the importance of charity as a fundamental element of human experience, and they will be encouraged over time to make links between that human experience and the belief that we are created in love by God, so that we might pass love on to others. In the discussion of divine pedagogy in a previous chapter we discussed the Catholic understanding that God is a mystery revealed progressively in various ways, not all at once, to the believer. With this in mind, students will not be expected to make deep theological links between human experiences and God at the outset of their schooling. They will, however, over the course of their education be continually invited to engage with theological understandings of the source of love and its significance for human life. These theological understandings have a cognitive dimension but are grounded in the experiences that students have of love in their families and even in the pastoral care afforded them at school. Staff reinforce Catholic doctrine with affective depth and meaning when they develop rich pastoral relationships with students, building a culture of care across the fabric of school life.

Justice

We have noted that charity expresses the Church's deepest nature, but it must be recognised that individual works of charity may simply reinforce and perpetuate injustice, rather than challenge the underlying social structures which oppress, exclude and diminish people. For example, the facility for people living with severe disabilities mentioned above was so understaffed that the residents were left inside all day with very little opportunity to interact with people. It is good that our students were able to visit the facility and provide some basic human interaction. Questions do, however, need to be asked as to whether we are satisfied as a society with these people being tucked away in institutions that are so under-resourced. As these social/structural questions are addressed, the curriculum moves from charity into justice.

Over the course of the past century the development of Catholic social teaching has highlighted the various ways in which social structures need to be critiqued by Catholics in the light of the Gospel. A very significant body of Church teaching has evolved around issues such as war and peace, poverty, human rights, the nature of the human person, family, freedom, marriage, the common good, work, politics, private property and the economy.

There is not the space in this chapter to grapple with this significant body of Church teaching, but I found an article written by Henry Novello helpful in terms of identifying some of the distinctive features that shape the treatment of each of the issues addressed by it (Novello, 2014). A key feature of Catholic social teaching is that it is grounded in an understanding that our humanity is assumed into the life of God by God becoming one of us in Jesus. Christians locate the sacred worth and dignity of each person in a theology of creation and the mystery of the incarnation.

A second feature of Catholic social teaching is the belief that freedom and truth are inextricably linked:

> *When human freedom refuses to be bound to the truth, it falls into arbitrariness and ends up submitting itself to self-indulgence, self-interest, and a self-love 'which refuses to be limited by any demand of justice' (Centesimus Annus, # 17). The error of detaching human freedom from the truth about humankind leads to devastating consequences that are apparent in the tragic series of wars, culminating in the Jewish Holocaust, that ravaged Europe in the twentieth century (Novello, 2014).*

A third feature of the Church's social teaching is the belief that God's Spirit is active in the realm of history and also in the lives of individuals and communities who are committed to building a better world. While Christians explicitly discern the promptings of the Spirit, Catholics recognise that all people of good will are open to the Spirit, even if they do not name their experiences in those terms. Catholic social teaching also refuses to identify the Realm of God with any political system or ideology such as capitalism or socialism. Marxist ideology is criticised because it absorbs individual freedom into the collectivity, and liberal capitalism is criticised for absolutising private property over the inalienable dignity of humanity as created in God's image. Any improvement in the common good here and now is always understood as a foretaste of the kingdom that is partially in our midst now but not fully arrived until death and sin are no more.

An issues-based approach to learning

Australian research confirms the value of an issues-based approach to learning. Hughes (2007) found that young people enjoy considering issues, as long as they were not told what they should believe. Many teachers take an issues-based approach to the curriculum because they believe young people engage more readily with issues than they do with abstract concepts or beliefs. Part of the skill of teaching is to know how to work with an issue to address educational outcomes that transcend the issue at hand. For example, capital punishment can be studied as an issue on one level, and on another level students can be invited to reflect on the sacredness of all human life, including the human life of a person who has committed reprehensible crimes.

Crawford and Rossiter (2006) report that young people will resist pedagogical strategies that they believe are seeking to change their beliefs or behaviours. Crawford and Rossiter argue that an 'issue-oriented' approach to studying beliefs and values helps to create a zone of freedom within the learning process. This zone of freedom is necessary because young people have come to expect that they have the freedom to explore viewpoints and explanations rather than having them imposed by a religious authority. This zone of freedom can be likened to the notion of 'frontier', which is presented in this book as the space between strangeness and familiarity where learning and growth of students can be maximised. Again, there are challenges and opportunities here for those who design curriculum and teach in a Catholic school if they are to create spaces where students grapple meaningfully with the issues in the context of a strong engagement with Catholic beliefs and values.

When an issue is the focus of the learning, rather than approaches that address the students' viewpoints directly, a certain distance is created that opens up a space (a frontier) where values and beliefs can be developed in the context of an engagement with an issue of interest to the students. Crawford and Rossiter argue that an issues-based approach is more fruitful than strategies which attempt to directly address beliefs and values. The issues-based approach, with its zone of freedom, does not reduce to a 'zone of escape'. Respect for the freedom of students does not mean that teachers need to avoid challenging or confronting their values or beliefs. Teachers who employ the skill of moderating described in the Pedagogy chapter avoid presenting a single path to truth; they create frontier spaces where students are challenged to identify the inconsistencies and contradictions within their own views and the materials being studied. Moderators know how to draw sensitively and appropriately from Catholic teaching during the learning process so that students are informed by Catholic beliefs, rather than being alienated by them.

Working in a frontier space

I recently attended a workshop for Catholic school leaders which focused on racism and the difficulty that Aboriginal and Torres Strait Islander people experience in weaving between the white and Aboriginal worlds. The presenters encouraged participants to combat racist attitudes by asking questions that open up spaces, rather than closing them down. The process in this workshop provides a good example of the frontier space that was the subject of Chapter 4. In the frontier space, people encounter each other in territory that is a meeting place, territory that is at once familiar and strange. If people are in territory that is too comfortable they will not be challenged to change attitudes which are unjust or oppressive. If the territory is too alienating, defences will be up and students will lack the openness required to consider new possibilities and perspectives. Educators who want to challenge their students to change inappropriate attitudes are skilled at opening up spaces that are both strange and familiar at the same time.

Teachers who are effective at realising justice outcomes in the curriculum are able to work in the frontier space where students are encouraged to move out a little from familiar attitudes and beliefs to consider new possibilities which may initially seem strange and alien to them. In a Dialogue School, Catholic beliefs and values will appear as landmarks in this frontier as issues are considered and new understandings and behaviours emerge. Dialogue pedagogies encourage students to befriend elements of the tradition which may initially seem strange or alienating.

reflection

▲ What are your thoughts on the view that an issues-based curriculum is one of the most effective ways to invite students to confront and change attitudes that are unjust or oppressive in some way?

▲ Do you open up a frontier space with your students as you encourage them to move out from established patterns of thinking and responding to consider new perspectives and possibilities?

▲ What do these spaces look like in your teaching, your classroom or the broader life of the school?

Is it charity or justice and does it matter?

Charity and justice are not exactly the same. Why is this distinction important? Sort through the following scenarios and decide which are examples of charity and which are examples of justice. Do this privately, then in pairs, and then in a whole group discussion. At the end of this task, explore why it is that our students need to know that both are necessary and why it is important to know the difference.

- Performing Christmas carols at a retirement village
- Involving children in a Mini Vinnies program
- Participating in a Clean Up Australia Day
- Lobbying government for Early Learning Centre funding
- Visiting and working with people in East Timor
- Teaching students about bullying and harassment
- Organising a can drive to donate food for a homeless persons' centre
- Writing to Council to seek a crossing for a dangerous stretch of road
- Signing a petition to parliament asking for Australia to accept more refugees each year
- Volunteering to sell badges during Catholic Charities week
- Ringing the local MP to protest how little Australia donates in Overseas Aid

reflection

- **STOP**: After considering this chapter, what worries or concerns us?

- **SLOW DOWN**: As we consider the approaches to charity and justice in our school, what would need to be addressed, clarified further in the light of reading this chapter?

- **OFF WE GO**: This chapter is a helpful resource for us to plan our educational programs on behalf of charity and justice. Why? Or why not? What are the opportunities and constraints that twenty-first century pedagogies present for realising the mission of the Catholic school?

Befriending Difference

The image below was taken during an 'intensive interaction' session in one of our Special Schools. It presents a beautiful example of the frontier space mentioned earlier in this book. A frontier can become a space in which people face each other and, to quote Jacques Haers again, 'encounter one another on a territory that is only partially familiar, that contains unfamiliar and as yet unmapped, unexpected features' (Haers, 2004). Special Schools open up frontier spaces in a unique way when staff and students make the commitment and take the time to create a meeting place between people who can come from very different places in their social, intellectual, emotional or physical worlds.

Intensive interaction is one of many strategies used to engage non-verbal students in processes of learning and communication. What I appreciated about this intensive interactive session was the creativity and sophistication of the teacher's engagement with the student. By covering his face with the hat and then taking it away, the teacher invited the student into a space of engagement, and the two of them communicated very powerfully and richly with each other without a word being spoken. An important feature of what unfolded was the agency given to the student to set the terms of engagement and to lead it herself. The hat was used as a tool to open contact, withdraw and re-engage during the interaction. I saw the open space as a frontier in which the student had an agency that was sustained over a significant time. This personal agency is all too often denied to students with special needs.

> **reflection**
>
> ▲ The Jesuits use the phrase 'cura personalis' (care for the whole person) to say something important about their approach to pedagogy. Cura personalis means that the teacher treats the student as being more than a receptacle for knowledge or skill. The talents, abilities, physical attributes, personalities, desires, heart, faith, and mind of the student are all seen as being equally worthy of the teacher's care and attention. What are strong examples of the care you offer students in your school and how do you see this care as an expression of your school's Catholic identity?

Faith, hope and love

How is intensive interaction an expression of a Catholic Special School's religious identity? Catholic schools do not have a monopoly on working intensively to connect with their students because it is to be hoped that all schools do this. One way of understanding the distinctive Catholic dimension of the practice in a Catholic school is to regard it through the lenses of the theological virtues of faith, hope and love. I was pointed in this direction by a comment made by one of the principals of our Special Schools, who said that being Catholic is meaningless unless it leads us to love one another. For him, the school's Catholic identity was authentic when loving relationships permeated the life of the school. We have already addressed this theme in our previous chapter on Charity.

The Catholic Catechism, in its discussion of the theological virtue of love, said that its fruits were joy, peace and mercy. Love demands kindness and 'fraternal correction' – it is friendship and communion. The notion of love demanding both kindness and fraternal correction is important, as we can grow as much from an act of kindness as we can from those who are prepared to correct us lovingly – and I presume in this context that fraternal correction is not just restricted to men who are brothers! 'Love is itself the fulfilment of all our works. Love is the goal; that is why we run: we run toward it, and once we reach it, in it we shall find rest' (St Augustine, quoted in *Catechism of the Catholic Church*, # 1829). There is so much here that helps us understand what lies at the heart of a living Catholic identity in a school, and these characteristics are writ large in our Special Schools. They are places that run on friendship, communion, and even fraternal correction and love.

Catholic schools are not the only schools where pastoral care is extended to the students, and we know that educators in the state and independent sectors lay equal claim to the quality of their pastoral care. A defining element for me in Catholic pastoral care is its source and motivation. Catholics feel called into loving, pastoral relationships because they believe in a God who is love, and they see that God reflected in their students, who are made in the image of God. While love is the greatest of the theological virtues, faith and hope also take us into the life of God. Faith is the virtue by which we believe in God. Faith therefore provides a foundation for the Catholic way of seeing the human person as being sacred and made in the image of God. When we see every human person in this way, we are uniquely placed to reverence each person, regardless of their intelligence or their value in economic or social terms.

Our Special Schools teach us in a unique way how to be Catholic in our time, but each of our schools has students with special needs who call us out into a frontier and challenge us to make our systems work for the students, not the other way around. Jesus reveals a God to us who has a special concern for children, for those who are in need of healing, on the edges or outcast for one reason or another. Jesus readily moved into frontier spaces with people, showed them compassion, encountered them deeply, and healed and challenged them, calling them out into new places. Jesus reveals a God who has made each person in sacred love – a God who is deeply at home in brokenness and resurrects the brokenness into new life. The God revealed by Jesus calls us to recognise the inalienable dignity and worth of each person, regardless of their social status or power or their worth as measured by economic or other metrics.

> **reflection**
>
> ▲ Reflect on a time when a student presented particularly challenging behaviours in your school. How did you cope with these behaviours as a community? What can be learned about the Catholic identity of your school through the responses that you made?

The people I speak with who work in Special Schools tell me that they are joy-filled places. One of them captured it well when she said to me: 'Our young people are some of the happiest people you could come across. They just enjoy the moment'. Intertwined with this joy, however, is the reality of grief and struggle. Parents are grieving as they let go of the hopes and dreams that they had for their children, and this grieving and letting go happens over a lifetime as various milestones are reached, such as school graduation or puberty or a marriage of a sibling. Of course, in the fullness of time, parents create new dreams for their children, but this is a process that unfolds in the context of grief, growth and hope. One of the parents put it beautifully at a conference: 'We shift our vision of our sons and daughters from impaired versions of us to fulfilled versions of themselves'.

Students with a disability can experience significant health issues or slip into patterns of behaviour that are violent or chaotic, and neither their families nor their teachers can understand why. One of the uplifting aspects of visiting a Special School is to witness the skill and commitment of the staff as they read 'problematic' behaviours in order to interpret and understand what the behaviour is communicating. Notwithstanding this skill and commitment, staff see on a daily basis that the lives of the students don't go according to the plans of those who care for them. There are moments when there are no answers and it can be hard to stay hopeful. Staff work intensively with the families and with each other at such times to keep the flame of hope alive. Once again, every school surely aims to be a place of hope, but the reasons for that hope vary from one school to another. An authentic Catholic school is grounded in a robust hope that is sustaining in times of abandonment. This hope finds its source in the grace of God, rather than relying solely on human strength (Catechism of the Catholic Church, # 1818).

Originally this chapter had been called 'Disability'. The name changed to 'Befriending Difference' because disability is a label that can be used to dishonour the personhood of some students and mask the fact that all of us have abilities and disabilities, and we spend a lifetime discovering them, reconciling ourselves to them and celebrating them with others who help us along our way. Our schools invite each of us into a successful place, whatever that success looks like given the unique context and circumstances that shape each of our lives. Success for each one of us always unfolds in the midst of brokenness, limitation, hope, failure, mystery and growth. Special Schools show us in a particularly striking way how our lives ebb and flow in a world that is charged with a grace that transcends human plans, skill and effort.

Befriending the vulnerable

Our Catholic faith calls us to appreciate the people who are vulnerable, marginalised or challenging in our school communities. Can you think of someone in your class or school community who is challenging, marginalised or vulnerable?

- ▲ Come up with a metaphor that reveals this community member as a gift to your classroom, your staffroom or the broader school community. Be creative as you develop this metaphor.

- ▲ What are the positive characteristics of your metaphor?

- ▲ What do these characteristics reveal about the community member?

- ▲ What are the negative characteristics of the metaphor?

- ▲ What do these characteristics reveal about the community member?

- ▲ What does your metaphor say about the broader school community that surrounds the community member and engages them in the life of the school?

- ▲ How might your school community develop a deeper appreciation of the gift that is the person you have been thinking about during this exercise?

A Catholic school's religious identity is so mission-critical that school leaders should do everything possible to strengthen it. Careful planning, appropriate resourcing, skilled delivery and rigorous evaluation are necessary if the strongest outcomes are to be achieved. Schools that are taking their Catholic identities seriously closely monitor their endeavours to ensure they are achieving the desired outcomes. The model below provides one way for a school community to be clear about the outcomes it is trying to achieve and the strategies being employed to achieve those outcomes.

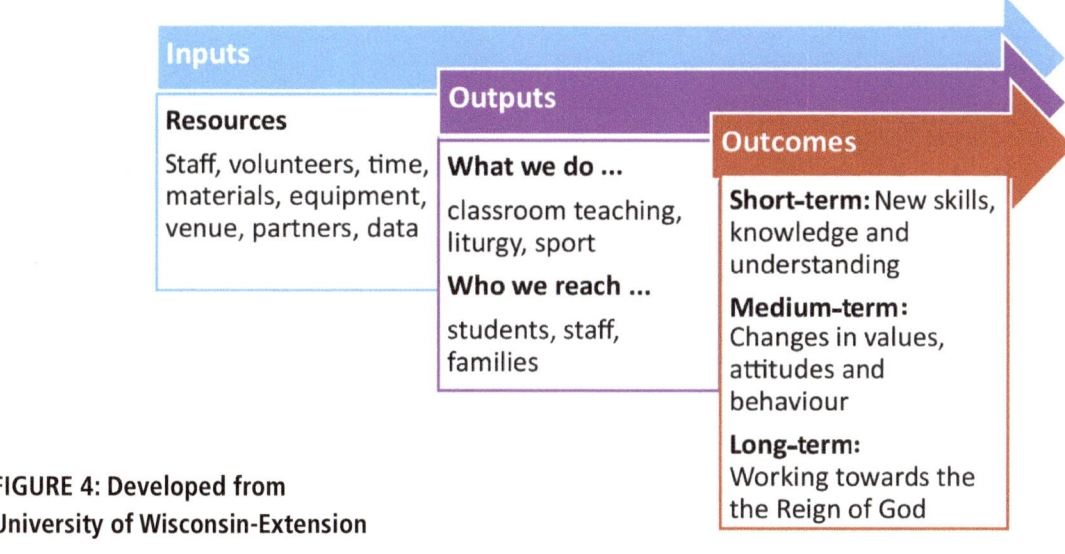

FIGURE 4: Developed from University of Wisconsin-Extension

I find it helpful to apply the model by working backwards from the right-hand side. What are the 'identity outcomes' that we are trying to achieve? Identity outcomes are formulated properly when they are shaped by the school's mission as well as the particular context of the school community. Outcomes can be broken down into short-term effects such as new knowledge – for example, about a Catholic belief – or a longer-term outcome such as a deep commitment to working for justice. It is recognised in this model that deeper outcomes often take longer to achieve. Once outcomes are clear, the focus can shift to the kinds of activities, interventions and audiences that might be associated with achieving the outcomes. Obviously these activities must be designed with the available resources in mind.

Most Catholic schools work hard to deliver religious programs that are plausible, but those involved must regularly ask themselves whether these programs are achieving the intended outcomes.

reflection

▲ What forms of evaluation do you use to review religious programs in your school?

One form of evaluation focuses on the *outputs*: Did all the programs run according to plan? Did the required number of students participate in them, etc.? Questions like these are important to ask and often relatively easy to answer. There are, however, deeper and more important questions to be explored, and the data for these questions is often harder to collect. Evaluations that consider whether the desired *outcomes* are being achieved provide stakeholders with evidence that the school's endeavours are achieving the results that were required. Program outcome questions are more important to answer because, ultimately, stakeholders want to establish that program outcomes are being achieved, not that staff busily delivered the program according to the plan.

Many religious outcomes are difficult to measure, but it is important nonetheless for school leaders to shift from 'I think we are going well' to 'I know we are going well because the evidence tells me so'. The archbishop in my diocese recently asked for a test to be developed that would give him good data on the religious literacy of students. During the development of the test we have had some valuable debates about the questions that should be included and the protocols that should apply to access to the data. The professional development associated with the design and administration of the test has also produced positive fruit, even ahead of the data being used to shape policy and practice in the Archdiocese.

Collecting the data

We have already considered two of the three research scales developed in a very fruitful partnership between the Catholic University of Leuven and the Catholic Education Commission of Victoria. The Post-Critical Belief Scale was considered in the Curriculum chapter and the Victoria Scale was considered in the Pedagogy chapter. Both of these instruments gather data that can be used to profile the religious options being taken up within the school. The data can be used by school leaders to identify issues with the school's Catholic identity and formulate strategies to address those issues.

There is not space in this chapter to examine the Leuven instruments in detail or the reports which are generated from them, but our experience in South Australia has been that the instruments have helped shift the identity conversation from anecdotes about the religious commitment and practice of students to a much deeper dialogue about the Catholic identity options being taken up within the school community. The Melbourne Scale is the third of the Leuven instruments, and it is discussed below because it provides another example of the way in which data can be generated to help deepen a school's understanding of its Catholic identity.

The Melbourne Scale's underlying theological and cultural foundations were developed by Lieven Boeve (Boeve, 2006) and subsequently operationalised into a scale by Didier Pollefeyt and Jan Bouwens (Pollefeyt & Bouwens, 2010). I have inserted my own labels in red in the diagram below for ease of understanding.

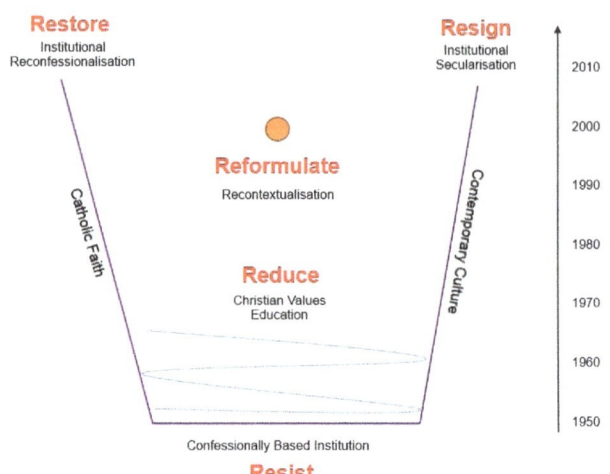

FIGURE 5: Developed from Pollefeyt & Bouwens (2010)

The scale assumes that as a consequence of the secularising trend in Western cultures there is a widening gap between our Catholic tradition and the broader culture in which a school's staff, students and their families live. This gap provides Catholic schools with some interesting options when it comes to the curriculum and pedagogy that is enacted in their schools. The technical terms used by the Belgian researchers for each of the identity options are printed in black in the diagram and I have included a verb in red to represent in layman's terms a key feature of the option.

Those who take the identity option at the bottom of the diagram see the school's Catholic identity as being unproblematic and therefore *resist* attempts to develop new programs or initiatives to address the secularisation of the school. Such leaders adopt a 'business as usual' approach to the school's religious identity because they either do not perceive that the gap between faith and culture is widening or, if they do see a gap opening up, they do not believe it has any implications for the Catholic identity of their schools. They resist any call for change.

Those who take the 'Reconfessionalising' option at the top left hand side of the diagram believe the school's Catholic identity needs to be *restored* because it has been eroded by secularisation. When the situation is assessed in this way, leaders seek to reassert or restore Catholic beliefs and practices. In some cases, leaders promote this 'restoration' as being deliberately 'counter-cultural'.

In a number of European countries, Catholic school leaders have adopted the 'Secularised Identity' option, represented at the top right of the diagram. Such leaders are *resigned* to the secularisation of the school, believing that this is inevitable given the strength of secularisation in their culture. When this option is taken, it is accepted that Catholic symbols, rituals, beliefs and practices will diminish and eventually disappear from the life of the school. The Catholic school simply becomes a brand within the public school system. I like the ambiguity of the word 'resign' for this option because I believe leaders who have become resigned to the inevitability of secularisation should resign from their roles!

A fourth option is the *reductionist* response represented in the lower middle of the diagram. Leaders here attempt cultural accommodation by heavily translating Catholic beliefs and practices into forms and expressions that sit as comfortably as possible in the wider social context. The strategy often emphasises values that are seen as being held in common between Catholicism and Australian culture. One common way this happens is when Catholic identity is built around abstract Gospel values divorced from the message and person of Jesus.

The final stance identified in the Leuven model is named 'Recontextualisation' (upper middle). Here leaders endeavour to *reformulate* Catholic beliefs and rituals into new expressions so they can be experienced as meaningful by community members. This option works from the premise that religious beliefs will be rejected by students, staff or families if they are imposed in a traditional form because the gap between the language of culture and the language of faith has become too wide. Faith (belief and practice) needs to find expression in new ways because of the new cultural contexts in which staff and students live – hence the need to 'recontextualise' Catholic beliefs, rituals and expressions.

The Leuven researchers suggest the option to recontextualise is preferred because in the face of advancing secularisation it is the most effective way to work at the interface between religion and culture at this time. As well as emphasising the importance of the development of new Catholic expressions, recontextualisation also highlights the unique and essential elements of Catholic belief and insists that these elements are respected as the new expressions are carefully developed.

Leaders who choose to recontextualise understand that attempts to impose dogmas or practices on people (restorationist approach) will be rejected by the students. Recontextualisers also understand that Catholic commitment is undermined, hollowed out and eventually rendered unviable when reductionist strategies are employed over time.

Analysing the data

Eleven schools have joined the Catholic Education Office in my state to survey their communities to ascertain which of these identity options seem to be operating in the schools and what an appropriate response might be to the situation the data reveals. We have formed a network to discuss the extensive report that each of us received from our colleagues at the Catholic University of Leuven, and many insights and understandings have emerged as a consequence of our shared reflection on our reports.

Taking action

For example, at the Catholic Education Office in my diocese we decided, after analysing the data from the instruments, that we needed to be more explicit in helping new staff understand what our prayers and rituals meant and how a person could find their place in them. We realised that in the past we have tended to hold back somewhat from being explicit about the Catholic content, shape and sources of our liturgy in order to respect the diverse backgrounds of the people coming to work in the Office. Now we are clearer about the need to be upfront and explicit about what we are doing and why, and we believe we are doing this in ways that respect the people we are dealing with.

The butterflies sculpture described in the Frontier chapter earlier in this book was developed in the context of a recontextualisation of Catholic faith. Parents met on a number of occasions with a sculptor over wine and cheese to share their stories and to reflect on the Catholic identity they were seeking for their daughters at the school. They workshopped their ideas with the sculptor and engaged with various passages of Scripture. The process culminated in the production of a cross adorned with three butterflies expressing themes of hope, resurrection and change and new life, which was particularly meaningful in the emergence into adulthood that is such a feature of life in the girls' middle school.

In another school, the Leadership Team presented parents with the data from the Leuven scales highlighting differences and similarities between staff, students and parents. This data enlivened a discussion with an artist where once again a sculpture was created that expressed something meaningful about the Catholic identity of the school. In this case it was a clay heart that is mounted prominently on a wall at the front of the school, making a strong statement to any visitor about the school's Catholic identity.

Another school embarked upon a significant renewal program in the area of staff prayer when they received their report, which indicated that 'most of the respondents report having a somewhat irregular prayer life'. This comment led to a realisation that there was a lack of dedicated prayer spaces in the school and to a further realisation that rote prayer was being over-used in the classroom, along with YouTube clips that were of limited formative value for the students. I mentioned in the Staff Formation chapter that staff were issued with a prayer journal and asked to bring it along to a 15 minute staff prayer session which was instituted as part of the staff meeting. The relational style of the leaders at the school allowed them to take this initiative in a way that led to life-giving outcomes for the staff and the students in the school.

DATA THAT LEADS TO ACTION
Collecting the Data

- Look at the religious tradition diagram in the Catholic Identity chapter and choose an element to focus on in this exercise. (The elements are represented in the circles inside the diagram.)
- There are many ways in which you might collect data about your focus element. For example, if you were to choose the Symbols element, you could walk around your school with a camera and take pictures of symbols that you felt said something about your school's religious identity.
- Your choice of data focus might be taken from a priority area in your school improvement plan or the strategic plan for your school.

Analysing the Data

- If you are undertaking this exercise with other members of your school community, you could share your images and begin to consider what questions would help unpack or synthesise the meaning of the data you have collected.
- It is important not to take images at face value and to find ways to look behind the image to see what it is saying about your school community.
- You might choose to ask how the image relates to another element of the tradition in the diagram. For example, you might ask what the symbol says about the prayer life in your school.
- Another approach would be to ask who the image includes and who it excludes. The only limits to the questions that can be asked are those of your imagination.

Taking Further Action

- Once you have collected the images and begun to analyse them, you can summarise what you have learned and what you would like to know more about and how you might undertake that further learning.
- Data collection and analysis should never be ends in themselves, the process should always lead to improved outcomes for students.
- How could what you have learned in this exercise lead to new questions or further research?
- It may also be that you already know enough to take action in some way to improve outcomes for students. You may choose to refer to the Program Logic Model at the start of this chapter and consider whether the outcomes you are considering are short, medium or long-term in nature. The links between your activity and the outcomes you are hoping for need to be carefully considered.
- This exercise has been designed to be undertaken in a relatively short amount of time. It could be broadened to include further elements of the tradition or expand the areas of inquiry or the groups within your community who are included in the process.

Doing Theology

We are nearing the end of our reflections on Catholic school identity, and it is time to bring the themes together into a conclusion. This final chapter focuses on the capacity to 'do theology' because that is one of the most critical things that a leader of a Catholic school must be able to do if the school is to have a vibrant and engaging Catholic identity. The premise of this book is that unless leaders are able to reflect theologically with their communities, their religious leadership will be severely stunted, as will the Catholic identity of their schools. Before proposing a model of doing theology, it is helpful to consider why it is so critical that leaders of Catholic schools are able to lead theological processes in their schools.

Leaders in Catholic schools need to be able to do theology

Each of the chapters in its own way has highlighted the importance of drawing deeply from the tradition so that new points of connection and access are created with members of the school community. Storytelling was emphasised in the Catholic Identity chapter as a way to build up a vital and meaningful Catholic identity in the life of the school. Important distinctions were made in the Jesus chapter between restorationist and reductionist approaches on the one hand and a recontextualising approach on the other. Restorationist approaches are rejected because they alienate students, whereas reductionist approaches hollow Catholic faith out by reducing the message and mission of Jesus to Gospel values. The recontextualising approach is preferred because it invites members of the school community to engage explicitly with Catholic beliefs to develop expressions that are meaningful at the same time as they are authentically Catholic. It is impossible to engage in this process unless one is able to do theology.

The Frontier chapter emphasised the importance of opening up spaces of encounter where rich Catholic expressions can be created between people who are familiar with the tradition and those who are living in worlds that initially seem quite foreign and remote from Catholic beliefs and practices. The remaining chapters

FIGURE 5: Adapted from Elizabeth Davis et al., eds., *Fire Cast on the Earth – Kindling: Being Mercy in the Twenty-first Century*, International Mercy Conference 9-12 November 2007 (©2009 the Mercy International Association).

in the book opened up similar themes of creativity, authentic engagement and the development of new points of access and connection with the tradition for community members. These themes of creativity, engagement and development rely upon a capacity to do theology, and they have played out in various areas of Catholic identity which have included Liturgy; Curriculum; Pedagogy; Staff Formation; Ecological Conversion; Family, Parish and School; Charity and Justice; Befriending Difference; and Data and Planning.

A method of doing theology

If new points of connection and access to the tradition are to be created, those who lead Catholic schools need to have a method which keeps them engaged with the tradition at the same time as they are immersed in the meaning of the lives and cultures of members of their school communities. This process of drawing from the tradition and creating culturally resonant meaning is essentially a process of doing theology.

Many leaders in Catholic education have tended to see theology as a product created by professional theologians and learned by those who study theology – rather than an activity which might be undertaken by lay people as they make sense of and respond to the ordinary issues of life.

It is critical, however, as Catholic school leaders that we understand we have to reflect theologically ourselves if we are to live up to what is required of us in our role as Catholic leaders. Without the capacity to do theology in the middle of our professional practice, it is simply not possible to recontextualise Catholic beliefs and practices in any meaningful way. There are many methods for 'doing theology', and the one presented here is offered because it is being used successfully by a number of leaders in the sector I work in. There are many other methods that have similar features to the process described here. The important thing is not that people follow this method, it is that they have a process that makes sense and works in terms of drawing deeply on the tradition and staying engaged with the lives and cultures of the members of their school communities.

The method has been tried by school leaders, and they find it refreshing. They believe the method has opened up a more explicit engagement with Catholic symbols, beliefs and rituals, and they like the deep listening that is entailed in the method. Unless leaders are able to find ways to do theology, their schools quickly become religiously arid places. The example below is taken from a doing theology workshop and illustrates how the process was used to deepen understandings of Catholic identity issues.

A number of school leaders recently participated in a workshop to develop their capacity to do theology. One of the principals had agreed to offer the group a situation in her school that would benefit from some shared theological reflection. She told us about a Year 6 student whom she called 'John' who was 'very challenging in many ways' and who had been diagnosed with a range of learning and behavioural difficulties. He was significantly overweight, had coordination problems, very poor social skills and no friends. John's behaviour had been deteriorating for some time, and after a very disruptive incident in the playground involving numbers of students and staff, parents of other students began to complain via email and other means about John's impact on their own children's schooling experience. They said things like: 'We pay school fees for a private education, John should be asked to leave the school. We don't care what his special needs are, he should not be with our children'.

Naming the experience

The group spent some time listening to the principal describe John's experience at school and the impact he was having on others. We listened deeply to what was being said. There were some good silences and a number of questions for further information or clarification. As we engaged in this process of deep listening and clarification, we were 'naming the issue' and undertaking the first phase of the doing theology process. In terms of our earlier reflections, this phase of the process could be described as entering the 'frontier'. The frontier is a place where people encounter each other, where we move out from our own settled territory to encounter the Other on his or her own terms, rather than conquering them with our own way of seeing the world.

Analysing the context

When we began to consider what might be causing John's behaviour we were moving into the second phase of the process where we had the opportunity to draw from relevant research to understand what was happening underneath the behaviour. Some reference was made to Choice Theory in this case, but we could easily have appealed to other social or psychological theories. Doing theology is more than sharing impressions or thoughts as they come to mind in a stream of consciousness. The process is only authentically undertaken when it is informed by appropriate data, analysis and research. While the process of doing theology is grounded in relevant theory and data, it is also illuminated by the light of faith. We reflected in the Curriculum chapter that meaning is created by entering a critical space but not by staying in that space. The critical phase entails an engagement with relevant theory and critical thinking, but the critical phase is a wayside stop, not a final destination. Paul Ricoeur framed the meaning-making process as being one of engaging critically, then moving into a new post-critical appropriation (a second naïveté) where the new meaning is informed by what was learned in the critical engagement, but not defined by it.

> **reflection**
>
> ▲ How deeply do people listen to each other and discern issues as decisions are made in your school?
>
> ▲ How effectively do you draw on research and data to inform the decisions that you make?

Dialogue with the tradition of faith

The third phase of the process of doing theology unfolds as a dialogue with Catholic beliefs and practices. One of the people who teaches this method uses Gospel images such as the treasure chest or the deep well to describe what the tradition of faith means for Catholics. Our tradition is a way of reading life that has many layers and levels of possibility and treasure. A deep well of knowing and wisdom has developed over 2000 years as a rich heritage of Christian belief. It is a wonderful, life-giving resource for life. The deeper chance you get to engage with the tradition, the more you know the reality of it.

We used the Parable of the Lost Sheep in this workshop to begin engaging the tradition explicitly in our process of theological reflection. The image of the shepherd leaving the flock to find the lost one reflected a basic Christian belief in the sacred dignity and inestimable value of each human person. One of the group observed that it sounded like the lost sheep had mauled some of the 99 and that this was not a one-off situation and a few of the sheep were threatening to leave the flock. This kind of intelligent and creative engagement with the tradition is a rich and fruitful part of the process of doing theology.

In terms of our earlier reflections in the Pedagogy chapter, the engagement with the tradition provides an example of moving from being a Colourful School to a Dialogue School. In the Colourful School, viewpoints are exchanged and dialogue occurs, but there is no deliberate engagement with Catholic symbols and beliefs. In the Dialogue School, the 'treasures' of Catholic faith are intentionally, appropriately and systematically drawn upon in the life of the school. Similarly in our Data and Planning chapter, we explored the need to 'Recontextualise' Catholic faith. Catholic faith is born again in every generation as Catholics make sense of their life experiences by drawing deeply from the wells of Catholic sacraments, teachings, symbols and stories.

Sometime after the workshop I asked participants to tell me what the Dialogue with Tradition phase was like for them. We agreed that every leader of a Catholic school would draw implicitly from the tradition in their outlook and daily practice because they have integrated Catholic beliefs and values over a lifetime. We also agreed that it was important periodically to engage explicitly with the tradition and to do so in a structured and disciplined way. One of the participants said that when we started drawing explicitly from the tradition we moved into a broader 'wisdom or heart space' rather than looking at John's situation more in terms of practicalities. Another felt that we moved into a space of hope when we started being explicit about our religious commitment and its implications for our work.

We agreed that doing theology together provided each of us with an explicit affirmation of our shared beliefs and values. One person summed it up by saying, 'I felt a strong sense of support because we come from the same values, the same tradition. The fact that we share these values at a deep level means that as educators we have something in common beyond merely practical issues that we focus on and resolve.'

Developing the vision for action

The fourth and final phase of the process entails developing a vision for action. Doing theology is not an exercise in armchair philosophising – it is a process that culminates in action. Sometimes the action is external in the sense that it results in a new behaviour or structure that is visible in the world. At other times the action is internal in the sense that it results in a new attitude or disposition to the issue being considered. The vision for action arises in response to a question such as: 'What will this look like, if we take account of what we have heard and seen, want and desire?' Those who do theology together can develop specific lines of action according to their particular context and circumstances. While it is important for the process to yield a coherent vision for action, individuals will apply that vision differently according to their own particular situation.

We saw in the Charity and Justice chapter that Catholic faith is not only about what happens in one's inner world. Catholic faith is ultimately an experience of

God's love calling us to enter into loving relationships with others and with the whole of creation. Catholic social teaching calls us to challenge social structures that oppress, exclude and diminish people. In his recent Apostolic Exhortation, Pope Francis issued a very strong call to Catholics to grasp the communal and societal repercussions of the Gospel. Francis notes that Christ redeems not only the individual person but also the social relations existing between people. He also notes that the Holy Spirit is at work in everyone, penetrating every human situation and all social bonds. Ours is a faith that leads to action. Ours is a faith that understands the Reign of God is central to the Gospel so that God's grace working in each person leads them to work for justice, peace and dignity. Finally, Francis notes that our faith is in a Christ who became poor and was always close to the poor and the outcast. Our Catholic faith leads us to be an instrument of God for the liberation and promotion of the poor, thus enabling them to be fully part of society (Evangelii Gaudium, 2013, # 187). There are profound implications here for the identity of the Catholic school, not only internally in terms of how members of the school community are treated but also externally in terms of the way the school positions itself in the world and the messages students receive about their place and vocation in the world over a lifetime.

reflection

▲ Do you have the skills and knowledge in your school to draw effectively from the Catholic tradition of faith as you formulate policy and enact it in the life of your school?

▲ Does the Catholic identity of your school lead you to care deeply about the poor in your midst (and those beyond the school gate) so that you take action in favour of liberation and healing?

The process of Doing Theology described above took approximately 60 minutes and is represented in the panel overleaf. 'School leaders' is a phrase used here to refer to anyone who has the capacity to influence the life of the school. Principals are school leaders but so are staff, students and their families in different ways. School leaders are busy people who work in the midst of fast-moving, 'hot action' of school life. The pace of schools does not allow every issue to be addressed by the discernment, deep listening, careful analysis, explicit engagement with the tradition entailed in this way of doing theology. While not every issue can be discerned by doing theology at depth, the school's Catholic identity relies on a commitment to finding time to do theology periodically in the life of the school.

An example of Doing Theology

This example is set in the context of a 60 minute, six member Leadership Team meeting at a school.

- A Leader was chosen to facilitate the 'naming and clarification of the issue' phase of the process – the Leader's job was to begin the process by inviting the group into a prayerful space and to facilitate the clarification of the issue being discerned.
- A participant had also been chosen prior to the session to share an issue of concern.
- The Leader invited the participant to describe the issue and then the Leader invited participants to clarify aspects which were unclear.
- The group was invited to consider what data or theory might inform their discernment of the issue.
- Another participant had agreed to choose a piece of Scripture before the session that would throw light onto the issue being discerned.
- Another participant had agreed to keep notes during the discernment process and presented key themes or insights which had emerged back.

Time	Action	Example	Comment
5 mins	The candle is lit and a prayerful space is created.	The Leader centres the group and reminds them that wherever two or more are gathered in Christ's name, he is there in their midst.	The Leader invites participants to leave behind the activities of their day and enter a space where they are explicitly aware of the presence of Christ in their midst.
15 mins	The issue/problem is named and clarified.	The difficulties currently being experienced by a child with learning and behaviour issues are described. The responses of the child's parents, teachers and other students and parents are also canvassed.	The Leader invites participants to ask clarifying questions once the issue has been shared. The goal is not to provide the answer but to listen deeply and discern what the issues are underneath what is being presented. Silence and space are seen as being desirable, allowing the movements of the Spirit to be discernible.
10 mins	Relevant theories and data are identified.	The child's issues are considered within a developmental frame along with some insights drawn from Choice Theory. The group identifies those situations where the child is behaving well and those where behaviour problems are manifesting.	The group critiques the theories and data currently being used to understand this situation. Do we know enough about what is really happening here? Alternative theoretical insights and data are considered.
10 mins	The group draws explicitly upon Catholic beliefs and values.	The Parable of the Lost Sheep is read (Luke 15:3–7) and the group considers what that text has to say to this situation. Initially the conversation is around the special claim that the 'lost' child has on the school. Some of the group begin to play around with the text, saying that this situation is not a one-off and that the 'lostness' of the child has become a pattern requiring a structural solution.	The Leader works to ensure that the Scripture is not artificially introduced into the conversation. Participants are encouraged to situate their interpretations of the text into the nuances of the situation as it has already been discerned and in the canvas of Catholic beliefs and worldview.
10 mins	Key themes and insights are named.	Insights relating the student's behaviours to underlying needs are shared by the note-taker. The responses of other students and parents are considered in the light of the school's mission.	The Leader seeks to ensure that insights which emerged in each of the phases of the process are remembered as the summary and thematisation is developed.
10 mins	A vision for action is developed.	The Leadership Team has a greater understanding of where the student is coming from in his behaviour and where others are coming from in their responses to that behaviour. The Year Level Coordinator will support the teachers while the principal decides what structural changes will set the student up for success.	Group members have different roles and spheres of influence and therefore their actions will differ accordingly. The Leader seeks to ensure that the vision for action is sharp and challenging enough to lead to specific action but broad enough to allow each participant to move forward into action that is relevant for their role.

In the Introduction to this book I mentioned that Jim and Therese D'Orsa have argued that school leaders can only make meaning in a Catholic context when they are able to 'do theology' with and in their communities (D'Orsa & D'Orsa, 2013). In a conversation with Jim about doing theology, he offered the following mnemonic as a way of summing up key elements of the process: CEDAR – Contextualise, Evaluate, Decide, Act, Review. The links with the method described in this chapter are obvious, as are the differences. There is no single way to do theology, but the elements of contextual understanding, analysis, engagement with the tradition, decision, action and review are all integral to the process. School leaders are encouraged to experience a method and experiment with it to discover what works for them in terms of engaging deeply with the tradition as lines of action are formulated in response to issues and opportunities as they arise in the life of the school. One of the most rewarding aspects of being a leader in a Catholic school is the challenge and the privilege of doing theology with members of the school community to ensure that the school's Catholic identity is living, vibrant and at the heart of what matters most in the life of the school.

Doing theology at your school

There are a number of entry points for school communities who want to explore and experience what it means to 'do theology'. One way to explore this model of doing theology is to use the data collected, analysed and synthesised from the previous chapter.

Naming the Experience: Refer to your data as you name the experience that you wish to be explored or further developed in the process.	
Analysing the Context: What research or theory will help you to understand the data that you have collected and deepen your understanding of the issue?	
Dialogue with the Tradition: Identify an element from the tradition that will illuminate the issue that you are exploring in this process. Draw as deeply as you can from the Catholic well: Scripture, Gospel images, a quote from a saint or from your school's Vision Statement.	
Develop the Vision for Action: Name the actions you will take to improve outcomes for your community in relation to the issue that you have raised. The outcome might be something relatively modest and short-term like new knowledge or it might be something more ambitious or longer-term such as a change in attitudes or behaviour.	

References

Arbuckle, G. (2013). *Catholic identity or identities: Refounding ministries in chaotic times.* Collegeville, Minnesota: Liturgical Press.

Benedict XVI. (2005). *Deus Caritas Est.* Retrieved from http://www.vatican.va/holy_father/benedict_xvi/encyclicals

Benedict XVI. (2012). *On the service of charity.* Retrieved from www.vatican.va

Boeve, L. (2006). 'The Identity of a Catholic University in Post-Christian European Societies: Four Models'. *Louvain Studies*, 31, 238-258.

Brueggemann, Walter (2010). *Genesis: Interpretation: A Bible Commentary for Teaching and Preaching.* Westminster: John Knox Press

Catechism of the Catholic Church. (1994). Homebush, NSW: St Pauls.

Compendium of the Catholic Church. Retrieved July 1, 2014, from Vatican Web site: http://www.vatican.va/archive/compendium_ccc/documents/archive_2005_compendium-ccc_en.html

Congregation for the Clergy. (1997). *General Directory for Catechesis.*

Crawford, M., & Rossiter, G. (2006). *Reasons for living: Education and young people's search for meaning, identity and spirituality.* Camberwell: ACER Press.

D'Orsa, J., & D'Orsa, T. (2012). *Catholic Curriculum: A mission to the heart of young people and Leadership for Mission: integrating life, culture and faith in Catholic education.* Mulgrave: Vaughan Publishing.

D'Orsa, J., & D'Orsa, T. (2013). *Leading for Mission: Integrating life, culture and faith in Catholic education.* Mulgrave: Vaughan Publishing.

Francis. (2013). *Evangelii Gaudium.* Vatican. Retrieved October 3, 2014, from http://w2.vatican.va/content/francesco/en/apost_exhortations/documents/papa-francesco_esortazione-ap_20131124_evangelii-gaudium.html

Haers, J. (2004). 'Religious Education as Conversation: Schools as Communities of Discernment'. In H. Lombaerts, & D. Pollefeyt, *Hermeneutics and Religious Education* (pp. 313-336). Leuven, Belgium: Leuven University Press.

Hughes, P. (2007). *Putting life together: Findings from Australian Youth Spirituality research.* Fairfield, VIC: Fairfield Press.

McEvoy, J. (2009). 'Proclamation as Dialogue: Transition in the Church-World Relationship'. *Theological Studies*, 30, 875-902.

Novello, H. (2014, Winter). 'Foundations of Catholic Social Teaching'. *Compass*, 48(2), pp. 22–27.

Pollefeyt, D. (2008). 'The Difference of Alterity: A Religious Pedagogy for an Interreligious and Interideological World'. In J. De Tavernier, *Responsibility, God and Society: Festschrift Roger Burggraeve* (pp. 305-330). Leuven, Belgium: Peeters.

Pollefeyt, D., & Bouwens, J. (2010). 'Framing the Identity of Catholic Schools: Empirical Methodology for Quantitative Research on the Catholic identity of an Education Institute'. *International Studies in Catholic Education*, 2(2), 193-211.

Pontifical Council for Inter-Religious Dialogue. (1991). *Dialogue and Proclamation.*

Reid, A. (2010). *The National Curriculum: the problems and possibilities for schools.* Paper presented at the Australian College of Educators, Pavilion on the Park, Adelaide, on Friday 12 March

Ricoeur, P. (1970). *Freud and philosophy: An essay on interpretation.* New Haven: Yale University Press.

Ricoeur, P. (1995). *Figuring the sacred.* (M. Wallace, Ed., & D. Pellauer, Trans.) Minneapolis: Fortress.

Taylor, C. (1991). *The Ethics of Authenticity.* Cambridge, Mass: Harvard University.

www.ingramcontent.com/pod-product-compliance
Lightning Source LLC
Chambersburg PA
CBHW061057170426
43195CB00024B/2985